IN MEMORY OF THE SIX MILLION
WHO COULD NOT TELL THEIR STORIES

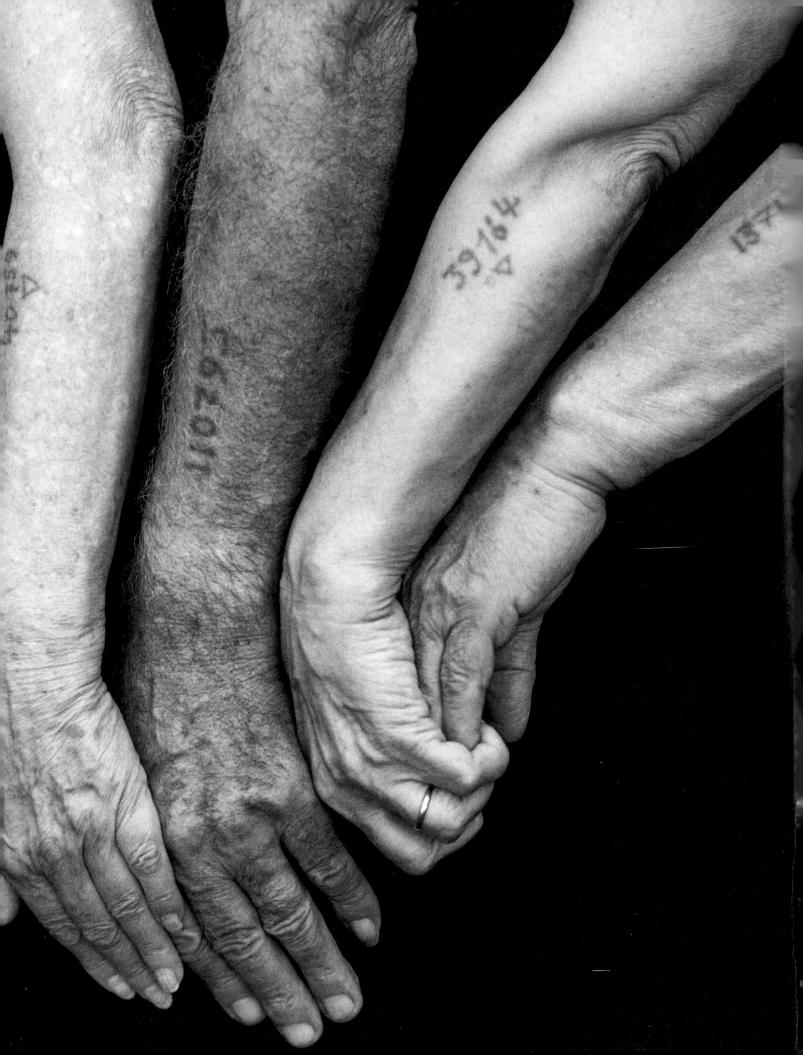

"WHEN THEY CAME TO TAKE MY FATHER"

VOICES OF THE HOLOCAUST

PHOTOGRAPHS BY MARK SELIGER

EDITED BY LEORA KAHN & RACHEL HAGER

INTRODUCTION BY ROBERT JAY LIFTON

ARCADE PUBLISHING · NEW YORK

FRED WOODWARD *Designer*

AMY GOLDFARB *Design Associate*

FIRST EDITION

Library of Congress Cataloging-in-Publication Data

When they came to take my father: voices of the Holocaust /
photographs by Mark Seliger : edited by Leora Kahn and Rachel Hager ;
introduction by Robert Jay Lifton. –1st ed.
     p.   cm.
   ISBN 1-55970-305-9
    1. Holocaust, Jewish (1939–1945)–Personal narratives.
2. Holocaust survivors–United States–Portraits.
3. Jews–United States–Portraits.
I. Seliger, Mark. II. Kahn, Leora. III. Hager, Rachel.
D804.3.W453 1996
940.53'18'0922–dc20   [B] 95-17852

Published in the United States by Arcade Publishing, Inc., New York
Distributed by Little, Brown and Company

10 9 8 7 6 5 4 3 2 1

SEM

PRINTED IN THE UNITED STATES OF AMERICA

"WHEN THEY CAME TO TAKE MY FATHER"

VOICES OF THE HOLOCAUST

THE TWENTIETH CENTURY has given us all too much opportunity to observe the human effects of mass killing and sustained cruelty. Yet there is still much that we do not understand about survivors of such experiences and their lives after their ordeals. Our ignorance has to do with an almost-insurmountable barrier between their extreme suffering and our own ordinary existence. Overcoming that barrier with Holocaust survivors requires us to take in both that suffering and the ways they have found to transcend it.

When body and mind have been assaulted, the self can either close down or open out—or, as is usually the case, do something of both. As observers of Holocaust survivors, however, we have not paid sufficient attention to the impressive capacity of some to absorb their pain—pain that can never leave them—and move beyond it into creative achievement and expressions of love.

My own dialogues, over decades, with Holocaust survivors seem always to reveal this double possibility. Survivors can remain bound to the suffering and its residual symptoms to the extent of near immobilization; but they also can acquire profound knowledge and insight.

The indelible imprint of death and suffering—cruel memories of the smoke or smell of gas chambers, the brutal killing of a single person, or the last moments with family members never seen again—can result in lifelong despair. But those searing images can also give rise to a form of death-haunted wisdom, along with life-affirming energies.

Similarly, survivors can become entrapped in self-condemnation—for not having done more to save the lives of others even when there was little chance to do so, or for having simply survived while people close to them died. But many transform this self-laceration into an assertion of moral principle, into active opposition to any form of genocide or killing. One can understand this process as part of survivors' lifelong struggle to reestablish a moral universe—for themselves and for the rest of us.

There are parallel tendencies in the overall realm of feeling. Many survivors are afflicted with strong tendencies toward psychic numbing, toward diminished capacity or inclination to feel. The most extreme and prolonged expressions of that numbing occurred in prisoners in Nazi death camps—those "walking corpses" of whom Primo Levi once wrote, "One hesitates to call them living: one hesitates to call

their death death, in the face of which they have no fear, as they are too tired to understand." But for most, a certain amount of psychic numbing was necessary for survival—numbing that was extensive but never total. One could maintain sufficient vitality of thought and emotion to evaluate danger and pursue whatever forms of self-protection and mutual help might contribute to survival.

Over subsequent years, many survivors engage in a process that they view as "learning to feel." They may need to hold on to degrees of psychic numbing in certain psychological areas to open themselves to ever-broadening experience in others; in effect, to undergo a partial inner death in order to protect and express more general assertions of life.

Survivors can, understandably, remain extremely suspicious toward other people and find difficulty in accepting friendship or love. To accept help or support can be perceived as a sign of weakness and a reminder of overwhelming helplessness in the past. But this pattern of suspicion of the counterfeit can be transformed into keen distinctions between the authentic and the inauthentic. Survivors know that their very presence can be a troubling reminder of extreme horrors that others would wish away; they seek recognition not only of their victimization but of their ability to cope with and live beyond that victimization.

Finally, survivors are thrust into a lifelong struggle for meaning. They must find some significance in their ordeal if they are to find meaning in the rest of their lives. Of great importance here is the impulse to bear witness, to take in what happened and make it known to others in all its terrible truths. Bearing witness can take the form of a survivor mission—a project that extracts significance from absurdity, life enhancement from the death immersion. For many, this project became the vast survivor mission of creating the state of Israel, but it could also take on more modest dimensions: reexperiencing love, creating a family, or finding satisfaction in professional achievement. Residual despair threatens, and is constantly warded off by, expressions of vitality.

The faces and narratives of the survivors in this volume tell us, loud and clear, of their rejection of a life of grief in favor of struggle toward realization and hope. They do not attempt to minimize or negate the full horror of the Holocaust; rather, they confront that horror in the service of a personal, and broadly human, future.

A LIFELONG QUARREL WITH G-D | *by Rabbi Arthur Hertzberg*

EVERYONE WHO HAS BEEN TOUCHED by the Holocaust—and what decent person has not?—has his own, personal quarrel with G-d, with other people, and with himself.

I have never found a way to absolve G-d of the crime of Auschwitz. I reached bar mitzvah in 1934, the year after Hitler came to power. Even as I participated in the ritual at the Hasidic synagogue in Baltimore, of which my father was the rabbi, I knew that I had come to doubt G-d. How could he let the Nazis win?

Inevitably, my troubles with G-d have only increased year after year. I find no help from those who say that he is a limited power, who encourages humanity to do good but is not responsible for the pain and evil in the world. "This-worldly," naturalist theologians, such as Mordecai Kaplan, were talking of a limited G-d—long before the Nazis appeared—as an answer to the problem of evil. But such a G-d is essentially created in the image of a fashionable preacher in a bourgeois synagogue or church; he has the power to exhort but not to command and, therefore, he has no responsibility for what is happening in the world.

The most elegant version of this idea—that God is not responsible for evil, and especially not for the ultimate evil of the Holocaust—was fashioned by Martin Buber in his *Eclipse of G-d* (1952). He invoked the cabalistic image that G-d sometimes "hides his face," that he absents himself from the world and so darkness rules, and turned this notion around; Buber suggests not that G-d had chosen to go away, but that some dark power eclipsed him for a time. But, as I once screamed at Buber himself in his home in Jerusalem, what right had G-d to go away, or to permit himself to be eclipsed, while my grandfather and all of my mother's brothers and sisters and their children were being murdered?

I have always been even angrier with those who find reasons to justify the ways of G-d, as he acted in the 1930s and 1940s. These theologies seem rooted in Scripture. In the historical books of the Bible, the usual explanation for the suffering of the Jews is that they had disobeyed the will of G-d and thus deserved to be punished. So ultra-Orthodox Jewish theologian Rabbi Joel Teitelbaum, the rebbe of Satmar, insisted in *On Salvation and Redemption* (1967). As his theory goes, the Jews were punished by G-d for the sin of Zionism—for refusing, as they had been commanded, to wait passively for the Messiah; the Zionists had rebelled against G-d by creating the state of Israel by their own hands. Many Zionists, including David Ben-Gurion, argued the opposite, that the Holocaust was the punishment of history on those Jews who refused to leave Europe

in time—long before 1933—for their own national home. That G-d, or his secular avatar "history," would let a million and a quarter small children, and five million of their parents and grandparents, die horribly because they were either too Zionist, or not Zionist enough, has always seemed to me to be an obscene idea. In my angrier moments, I have said, and not only to myself, that a G-d with such motives deserves to be defied.

A number of my friends who were firmly Orthodox before 1933 became fierce atheists. I have not joined them because I keep rereading the Book of Job. Every conceivable woe happens to this righteous man, Job. He rejects all the explanations that his solicitous friends try to offer him. Ultimately, he summons G-d to give him an answer. Replying out of the whirlwind, G-d offers Job no explanation, but he does not disclaim responsibility. "Where were you," G-d asks Job, "when I founded the world?" His powers are indeed unlimited, and he is never absent from the world, either by choice or because he is in eclipse. G-d simply asserts that there is meaning to the world, and even to Job's suffering, but it is beyond man's understanding. And yet, even as I read these verses over and over again, I keep asking the question, What about Job's children? Job survived the tragedy of their death, but could he ever forgive G-d?

Why G-d was silent from 1939 to 1945 will forever be a mystery. The disbeliever will insist that this silence proves G-d's irrelevance or his nonexistence; the believer will hold on to the faith that the world adds up, but only in the mind of G-d.

The conversation about the Holocaust that lives with me—and haunts me—was one that never took place. Rabbi Aaron Rokeach, the rebbe of Belz in southeastern Poland, lost his entire family—his wife and all his children and their children—in the Holocaust. He never again mentioned them, or even said prayers in any visible ritual in their memory. I was in his presence in Tel Aviv in the summer of 1949. I tried to get the rebbe to talk to me about my grandfather and my uncles, who had been his disciples and friends, but he simply did not respond, not even with a gesture. The dead were too holy, so his closest associates explained, to need words. The rebbe of Belz had accepted the tragedy, his and everyone else's, in silence—and he was rebuilding his Hasidic court in the Holy Land. Silence and rebuilding—that was how he spoke for his faith in G-d.

After a half century of thinking about the Holocaust, of hearing many stories, and of reading many books, I am left with a lifelong quarrel with G-d, and ambivalent relationships with the gentile world, with Jews—and with myself. Even though I was once overwhelmed by the silence of the rebbe of Belz, I cannot join him. I must light candles in memory of my family, and I continue to grieve over the horror of their deaths—but it is their *lives* that I want to remember. The Jew within me cannot forget the gas chambers, but what I most want to remember are the children who published a daily newspaper in Theresienstadt, the inmates of Auschwitz who held forbidden prayer services, and the heroes of the Warsaw ghetto, in the years before the revolt, who conducted schools in defiance of Nazi edicts. This is what I have learned from rereading the Book of Job on the aftermath of the Holocaust. After his disaster Job begat a new family, re-created his flocks and herds, and did good again to all who came into his sight. Job remembered what he had lost, but he did not simply continue to scream; he lived on.

The survivors did not dwell on death; they rebuilt life. This was the lesson they were teaching: a people must remember, but it cannot live on by making a cult of its woes. The faith of the Jews is not simply remembering the Holocaust; it is the Jewish religion, which—before and after the Nazis—reasserts the verse in Psalms, "I will not die, for I will live." Those who remained after the Holocaust, and their children and grandchildren, must live all the harder, and all the more decently, to carry on for every one of the unfinished lives.

Rabbi Arthur Hertzberg is currently a Bronfman Visiting Professor of Humanities at New York University and has previously been a faculty member of Dartmouth College and Columbia University.

"I HAVE TO GIVE THE RUSSIANS CREDIT: THE FIRST THING THEY REBUILT WAS THE OPERA HOUSE. THAT STARTED A NEW ERA FOR ME. THREE YEARS WITHOUT THE VIOLIN WAS A LONG, LONG TIME."

I THINK IT WAS around 1940. I already had my diploma from the Franz Liszt Academy of Music in Budapest. I was sent to a labor camp near the Romanian border, where I spent almost three years.

Once, after two and a half years in that camp, when we were being marched back from Stanislaw (Poland), a friend and I decided we had to take a chance and try to escape. During the march we slept outside in ditches, so late one night my friend and I snuck away from the group and went to a church a few steps away. We escaped to Hungary wearing priest outfits.

I returned to Budapest and survived with the help of Raoul Wallenberg at the Swedish embassy. By the time I arrived, the embassy was full; people were sleeping on the floor. I received a *Schutzpasse*, which made me a so-called Swedish citizen. But even with a *Schutzpasse*, leaving the building was a big risk—sometimes the Nazis accepted that piece of paper, and sometimes they didn't.

My job at the embassy was to work the telephone switchboard. The Hungarian Nazis, the Arrow Cross, were bombing the city continuously. One day in December 1944, they came into the embassy and took 200 or 250 people. This was supposed to be a Swedish sanctuary, but there was no such thing as law anymore. Whoever they took, they would shoot at the edge of the Danube; that was the usual procedure. I called the number I had in case of emergencies, and two hours later, every single person who had been taken was back at the embassy.

To this day, I don't know who was on the other end of the telephone, but whoever it was had power over even the Arrow Cross. That's how high an in Wallenberg had. He had contact with Adolph Eichmann, with everybody. He was simply not afraid. He went to the Hungarian-Austrian border and brought back hundreds and hundreds of people.

After this incident, the bombing intensified. Everyone just stayed in the basement. Toward the end there was house-to-house fighting to such a degree that the Germans would be on one side of the basement and the Russians on the other, and they would be shooting over all of us who were just lying on the floor. Then the Russians occupied the city completely.

I was still at the embassy when Wallenberg left. He always left with a backpack, always in a hurry, a million things on his mind, running and running and saving and saving. The day he left, we didn't know where he was going. Nobody knew what was going to happen.

I COME FROM A SMALL TOWN in Yugoslavia, about an hour from Belgrade, from a very wealthy family. We had a lot of property. I had everything a youngster could imagine, because I had a father who said, "Money is good for one thing only: to enjoy and to get what you want." When I finished school, my father sent me to Vienna to art school. I was there for just under a year. A few days after Hitler entered Vienna, I went home.

I told my father what I had seen in Vienna and begged him to leave Yugoslavia. He listened to me and cuddled me and then told me that I was home and everything was okay and I should forget about it. This man who I adored, I hated at that second. I realized then that we are made in a very interesting way. No matter how hard we try, we do not understand or believe anything unless we see it, touch it, smell it. The next year I went to Paris to finish school. Then I came home. Of course, I didn't do anything with my degree.

When Hitler entered Yugoslavia I remember standing in our yard when a German soldier, a young boy really, approached me and asked for a glass of milk. After we walked a few steps, I stopped and said, "You really shouldn't ask for milk from a Jewish girl's hand." The boy stopped and looked at me and said, "Oh, my goodness. You look just like everybody else!"

My father became a total vegetable. So whatever had to be done, I did. We escaped to Sarajevo, because I didn't want to be in a small town where I was Beck the Jew. My uncle lived in Sarajevo, so we felt kind of safe there. And then one night, my father and brother were taken.

I decided to go to the mayor to find out what had happened to them, but the Germans kept me at the police station. I was ordered to clean toilets, and when I asked this German officer what I was supposed to clean them with, he said, "With your bare hands. Do you understand?" And I said, "No, not at all." So he started to hit me, and I laughed. He asked me what I was laughing about, and I said, "You know, I can't understand. I'm a young lady. You are an officer, which means you are a young gentleman. How can you hit me?" And he stopped.

But I was in the hands of a real sadist. The officer made the sergeant at the station get on a bicycle and tie me to a rope and I would have to walk through town like that. I had been at the station for three and a half weeks when one day, I was standing on top of a ladder cleaning the windows and a German officer walked by. He looked up and said, "What are you doing up there?" "Don't you see? I am cleaning the windows," I said. He told me to come down and then looked at my hands and said, "You don't exactly have the hands to clean windows." He asked me what I was doing there, and I told him I had come to see the town mayor on an important matter but that I had never even gotten to him because I had been forced to work here.

He went into the station with me and said, "I need her, she speaks German and Serbian. Can I borrow her for a few days?" And they had to comply because he was a higher-ranking officer. He said, "Go to the town mayor. I will vouch for you." And when I thanked him and asked him why he did all that, he said to me, "Es ist meine Pflicht als ein deutscher Offizier, als ein Mensch, den anderen Menschen zu helfen. Und glauben Sie mir bitte, daß jeder deutsche Offizier so denkt." which means: It is my responsibility as a German officer, as a human being, to help the next human being. And please believe me that every German officer thinks this way.

My mother and I then made our way to Italy, where we were interned on an island–a sheer dream under the circumstances. When the Axis powers broke apart, the Italians ran home and left us there. We were in no-man's-land. The partisans came down from the mountains. They had nothing either. For four months, we went from one island to another in fishing boats. We finally landed in Bari.

That's where I found out my father and brother had been killed. They had been sent to Yasenolitz in Croatia. You have no idea what hope does for a human being. I survived because I had the hope that my father and brother were going to come back from the concentration camp. And I tried everything possible to save them. I collapsed totally when I found out they were dead. I even tried to commit suicide. I had turned into a different person, full of hatred and bitterness. And I hated myself for it, but I couldn't help it. When I didn't die, I gave myself a year. And I told myself that if I can make a human being out of myself, I will continue. And if not . . .

My mother was deeply religious, so that helped her. I wasn't, from the time I was a child. In my mind, G-d was like Clark Gable. I admired my mother's faith and I was actually envious of it. But belief is not something that can be taught. You either have it or you don't.

"I FIND THAT THE BEST ONES WENT, AND WE WHO SURVIVED ARE THE WORST. MY FATHER AND BROTHER COULD NEVER SURVIVE, NOT EVEN A DAY. THEY WERE FINE, SENSITIVE, IDEALISTIC."

~BIMBA BECK

"THE SIGN OF A FREE MAN IS BEING ABLE TO KEEP YOUR HANDS IN YOUR POCKETS."

~LEE BERENDT

WHEN THE GERMANS CAME into my hometown of Sompolno, Poland, in September 1939, the Jews were ordered to assemble in the town square. Once we were there, the German officer in charge said to us: "Jews, your good life has come to an end. You know that you have insulted the Führer. Work you must. You will not be remunerated. And your complaints you can bring only to Jehovah in Jerusalem."

One of the hardest things to imagine about Auschwitz is that it was not constant slaughter for those selected to work. A prisoner was worked until he or she was of no more use to the German state. The daily routines of Auschwitz, horrible as they were, became the daily routines people got used to living by. We still got up, worked, went to sleep, and dreamed and hoped and talked about what might happen in the future. You just kept on going, kept on living, even on the threshhold of hell. . . .

There were two men to a bunk, and each bunk was a triple bunk. Every morning, twelve men emptied into an area that measured about six feet eight inches by four feet. When the morning bell sounded at 4:00 or 4:30 A.M. and the lights came on, the top occupants had to throw their clothes down onto the floor and make their beds in the most expeditious manner possible. The men in the middle beds had to dress themselves. And the men in the bottom beds had to run with their clothes out into the open and get washed and dressed. When the top occupants finished making their beds, they went out and washed and dressed themselves and the middle occupants had to make their beds. And so on.

We had plaid blankets. Each of the blankets had a mark in a certain spot guaranteeing that we would make the beds absolutely straight and level. Once made, the beds could not be disturbed. If a speck of dust was found, beatings would ensue.

When everybody was dressed and the bunks made, the day began. We were driven out into the open, regardless of the weather, and counted. Each barracks had a crew of workers—cleaners, dusters, bed checkers. After the barracks were cleaned, we were given bread and coffee in our bowls, which, together with our spoons, we had to keep immaculate and carry with us at all times. After breakfast, we assembled in front of the barracks to march out to *Zahl-Appel* (the gathering place).

From there, we marched out of the camp to the central shop, where we were broken up into our work subgroups and assigned our workplaces for the day—always in I. G. Farben building sites outside the camp.

We were never marched out if it was too cold for the camp musicians to sufficiently warm up their hands so that they could play their instruments. No music, no marching. The SS's favorite song seemed to be "Roll Out the Barrel."

The days at Auschwitz centered around being counted. We were counted a minimum of fourteen times a day. We had a saying amongst ourselves: "Counted like gold, treated like shit." The major counting of the day took place at sundown at the *Appel*, after we had completed our work. Any executions or punishments were carried out at this time. Then we were marched back to our barracks in order to wash up and get ready for our main meal of gruel and bread. After assembling again, an inspection was done—all our shoes had to be cleaned, and all of our uniform buttons had to be in place. Anything less resulted in a beating.

All those selected for the gas chambers had to assemble opposite block 12. The adults usually took it stoically. They were resigned to their deaths, knowing that their misery and suffering would soon be over. But late in 1944, as I stood at rigid attention, a group of Hungarian Jewish children were selected. Out of the corner of my left eye, I saw how young boys were looking for solace from elders similarly selected. They wanted to have their hands held. These children hadn't really lived, and they knew that they would soon die. Being selected for death was something they couldn't yet fathom. . . . As hardened as I was, an "old-timer" in the camps at the age of twenty-one, many a time I was moved to tears. I was helpless.

In the late spring or early summer of 1944, I was transferred from the 23rd Commando, which worked in carpentry, to the 147th Commando, which worked in the chemical warehouse. Since I was now in a higher-numbered commando, I had about thirty to forty-five more minutes to get ready before the commando assembled in the morning. I used this extra time to visit people I knew—the old-timers. Each day, we took an inventory of who was still around from our original group—the 142,000 who had come to Auschwitz in the summer of 1943. We discussed politics and the latest war developments. We could hear the booming of the Russian guns on the eastern front. On a clear day, looking south, we could see the peaks of the Tatry Mountains on the horizon. That was where we knew freedom was, where we knew the partisans were roaming, and perhaps where G–d had sneaked in, too. The place where we were, G–d overlooked or was ashamed or afraid to enter.

It was the hope of almost everybody in the camps to live just one day to see the Germans beaten. It was my luck to survive. I went back to Sompolno after the war. It was the thing that drove me to survive the camps—vowing to go back to my hometown and slam the door behind me.

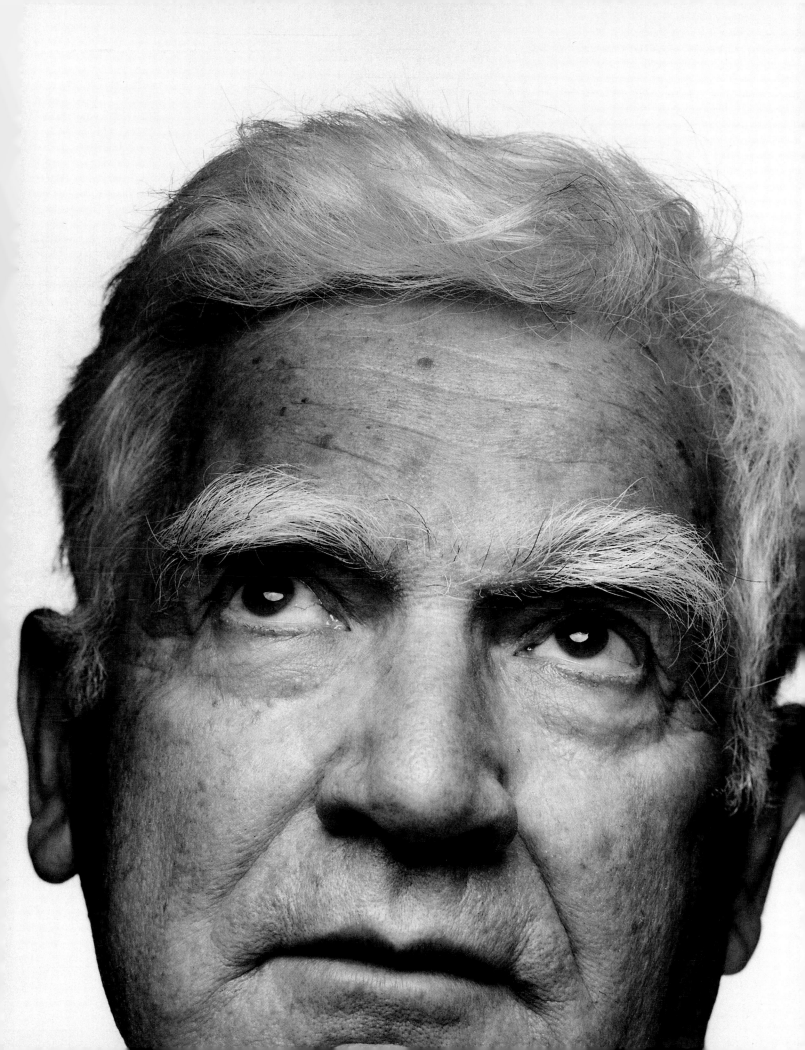

LIVIA BITTON JACKSON | *Birthplace* Chamorein, Czechoslovakia

Auschwitz survivor | *Occupation* Professor of Holocaust studies at the City University of

New York | *Current residence* New York, New York

THE SELECTION AT AUSCHWITZ was quite automatic. They didn't give us time to think. It was like being on a moving conveyor belt, rushing forward. When we reached [Josef] Mengele, the line slowed somewhat and we were immediately separated into two groups. Mothers with their children, older people, the handicapped, went immediately to the left and to the gas chambers. To the right went people above sixteen and below forty-six.

My mother and my aunt and I were locked arm in arm. We were already marching to the left when Mengele noticed my hair. I was very tall for my age. And I had greenish eyes and very light blond hair, very thick and straight and long, which I wore braided. It was quite unusual.

I had the ideal Aryan look, what Hitler was breeding for. So when he noticed me in the line he reached with his stick and he said, "You, stop. You come back here." He took one of my braids in his hands and he said, "What beautiful golden hair you have." His tone was very gentle. "Are you Jewish? Is that your mother?" I told him it was. So he called my mother back and he said, "Now the two of you, you go this way." And my aunt started to cry. And she said, "Lorika, don't leave me." She was panicky. My mother stopped and turned to Mengele and said, "Please let me go with my sister. She needs me." And he said, "No, you go with your daughter. She needs you more."

My mother became very sick and was taken to the sick barrack. I wanted to see her very badly and find out how she was doing. I took a chance and circled the barrack until I found a hole in the wood. I called to her and from her response found out where she was. She put her head against the wall so we could talk to each other.

One day I was caught when a guard came. I thought I was going to be executed, but I was very lucky and instead only received a punishment. Outside the command barrack there were these sharp, dark pebbles like the kind of gravel you see between train tracks. I had to kneel on those pebbles for twenty-four hours without food or drink. And I was very grateful for this. Because I lived. This is my memory of those hours:

The command barrack is near the entrance of the camp at a distance from the other barracks. I'm kneeling, facing the fence. Beyond the fence there is a road flanked by barbed wire on the far side. Beyond that fence I can see endless rows of barracks identical to the ones in our camp.

From the spot where I kneel I can look down the road both ways and see infinite rows of barracks like ours in every direction. The immense proportion of Auschwitz strikes me for the first time. Never before have I had a chance to see this. An array of identical low gray buildings neatly stretching as far as the eye can see. A world of barracks and barbed wire. Groups march on the road. Men in striped uniforms. Trucks and military cars. Women drawing carts with large cauldrons; others carrying cauldrons on wooden bars across their shoulders. Women and men in varying degrees of malnutrition.

There are some who can barely walk, and it seems as if they will collapse any moment. Others seem nothing more than darkened skeletons, yet they walk without faltering. No one looks to the side. Not one of them notices me.

Suddenly a marching column appears on the road. Men and women and children marching on and on. They're marching in rows of five. Women with their hair, with colorful clothes, some with hats on. Men and young boys and little children. A little girl clutching a doll. Their faces are white, without blisters and sores. They walk fast, breathless, afraid. But they walk like people, nervous and alert. They are not robots animated by an unseen force. They are people moved by a force within. They must be a transport just arrived. They still wear the facial expression of the free. They have not yet acquired the inmate posture. How different they are.

Some glance at the barbed wire fence as they walk. Several look at me. A young woman even smiles at me. I take a chance. I call out to her in German, "Where are you from?" "From the ghetto of Lodz." "Did you say Lodz?" "Yes, Lodz." "You came now from Lodz?" "Yes, we're just arrived." The last words she shouts from a distance; she's marching on. A little boy drops his clown. It's a dirty yellow. He's about to pick it up. The roar of the motorcycle approaches. An older boy gives a tug and the little boy marches on without the clown. The clown remains at the dusty roadside.

The column marches on and on, row after row after row. Now they are gone and all is quiet again. The dust settles. The clown lies still in the sunshine. My dear G–d, have mercy on the little children. The little boy with the doll and all the others. All the others.

These families are all together. I know they have not undergone selection. They are being taken directly to the gas chamber. It is August 1944, and I am surprised that the Lodz ghetto is just now liquidated. The Polish Jews had been in Auschwitz at least two years ahead of us. And before Auschwitz they were taken to Treblinka and Majdanek.

I saw the Lodz ghetto arrive in Auschwitz. And I know that the bulk of them went straight to the gas chambers. Because I saw it that day, kneeling on those stones.

"I RECENTLY MET A MAN WHO BURIED MY FATHER IN BERGEN-BELSEN, AND HE TOLD ME SOMETHING THAT I DIDN'T KNOW. THE WEEK BEFORE MY FATHER DIED OF THE RAVAGES OF STARVATION, HE SAID, 'I HAVE ONLY ONE REQUEST; TRY TO BURY ME ACCORDING TO JEWISH RITE.'

THE BARRACK FLOORS WERE EARTH.
WHEN THEY COULD, THEY
BURIED PEOPLE INSIDE
THE BARRACK SO THAT THE

NAZIS

WOULD NOT KNOW
THIS PERSON HAD DIED
AND TAKE HIM AWAY AND
THROW HIM IN THE
OVENS. THEY WERE LUCKY.
THERE WAS NO ROLL
CALL THE DAY AFTER
THEY BURIED MY FATHER."

~LIVIA BITTON JACKSON

"I'M LOOKING FOR THE POLISH GIRL
WHO GAVE ME HER PAPERS FOR FIFTY YEARS.
I PAID HER FOR THE PAPERS,
BUT HOW MUCH IS A LIFE WORTH?
THOSE PAPERS GAVE ME THE BACKBONE
TO DO ANYTHING."

~SANDRA BRAND

I HAD BEEN A REBELLIOUS CHILD. I couldn't stand the very strict rules of my father, who was a Belzer Hassid. All the Jews in my little town hated me because I did whatever I wanted. The girls my age were jealous; I think they also would have liked to do what they wanted, but they didn't dare. As a child I wrote poetry. And my plan and dream was to become a writer. But when I was eighteen I got married, and when I was nineteen I had a child, and two years later Hitler marched his troops into Poland, into Niemirow, the little town where I was living. Our plans and dreams were shattered.

My husband was a lawyer, and he had an office in Niemirow, but when the Germans came in, they closed it. Eventually, he went to Zlatov to live with his parents. When the Russians came in, I was told that we were in danger because my father was a member of the bourgeoisie and my husband was a lawyer. So I went to Lvov with my three-year-old child and got a job at a department store, and my husband came shortly after.

When the Germans attacked Russia, in violation of their pact, the Germans gave the Russians permission to do to the Jews whatever they wanted for eight hours. But these eight hours spilled over into three days. That's when I had the idea to get false papers and go to another city where nobody knew me, and to pretend to be a Polish Catholic woman. We decided I should go first and get a job for my husband as a bookkeeper, also under a false name, and find our child a place with a Polish family. We felt we couldn't all live together; once one was caught, the other two would be as well.

I decided on Warsaw. I registered with the local police under the name Cecilia Sasha Szarek. With help, I got a job as a translator with a German company, Vinetta, that imported merchandise from the ghetto. Equipped with that beautiful German *Arbeitskarte*–a working card–I went back to pick up my husband and child from Lvov; but within those six weeks there had been an action. They had already been deported.

Desperate and alone, I went back to Warsaw, where I discovered that false papers were not a passport to life. I had to watch myself day and night. I had to lie from morning until evening; it was so difficult that, once the war was over, I wouldn't lie even if it might bring me great benefit. But for three years I lied, very successfully, it seems.

One day two German soldiers came through the back door of the pensione in which I lived. They said, "There is a Jewess from Lvov in this apartment, and we've come to arrest her." I immediately knew they meant me. I went with them to the landlady, and the landlady said there was no girl from Lvov there. They looked into my pocketbook and found a photograph of my husband and child. About my husband they said, "This is a Jew." I denied it, of course. They took my jewelry and left, saying that they'd come back tomorrow. I went to the bathroom, tore the photograph apart, threw it into the toilet, and flushed. I felt like I had murdered my child. I saw half his face floating there on the water, and reached out for it and grabbed it.

The Ukrainians told me to go to the police to file a complaint, and I was afraid not to go, because who doesn't want to get their jewelry back? The local police said it wasn't their matter and sent me to the German police. So I had to go to the lion's den–to the Kriminalpolizei. I told a German officer what happened, and he said, "We'll do our best to find these perpetrators, and you'll hear from us."

It turned out the two robbers had already thirty other robberies on their conscience, and this German criminal police officer got a promotion for breaking the case. He came to my office to return one of my pieces of jewelry and invited me to go with him to a restaurant to celebrate. What to do? Should I go out with a German?! If I don't go, maybe he'll take revenge. So I went. And that's how it started. His name was Rolf Peschel.

Rolf started coming to the restaurant where all the workers at Vinetta ate–meals were part of our wages. So I stopped going there. I was afraid he would find out that I was Jewish. All of the girls were flirting with him–he was a good-looking man–but he always asked for me.

One day, a Jew who had the right to work on the Aryan side came to me and said, "They arrested twenty-five Jews who work for our company, and they are to be deported. I heard you have a friend. . . ." Now, this man didn't know I was Jewish. Nobody knew. So I said, "Me? Why do you expect me to help Jews?" I had to protect myself. My heart went out, but I pretended. And he said, "Jews are people too." I thought I would burst into tears.

So I called Rolf and said I wanted to meet him. He said he had nothing to do with that sort of thing, but he had a friend who had some connection with a German by the name of Brandt who was near the Umschlagplatz in the ghetto, and he said we should go there; he wanted me to come with him.

We did, and while Rolf went over to talk to the Germans, I waited a little distance away. From where I stood, I could see a group of Jews marching in a row. It was raining. One woman went up to the Germans and fell to her knees, asking for something, I don't know what. Then I heard a shot, and she fell to the ground. I probably cried out, unaware of myself, and two Germans came up, and said, "You are Jewish." I said I wasn't, that I was there with the criminal police officer. But they arrested me and took me to a building in the vicinity. I thought that Rolf Peschel sent them—that he found out that I was Jewish, and he sent them to get me. But before very long, Rolf came in, pale, and said, "If something would have happened to you I would never have forgiven myself."

When we went back out, Rolf said, "Workers of Vinetta, line up, I can take you out of the ghetto." But they didn't get up. They thought it was another German trick. So in Polish I said, "Get up, this German has a permit to get you out of the Umschlagplatz, out of the ghetto." They looked at me, this blond, and clearly thought I was in cahoots with this German. They wouldn't get up. I was desperate. I saw one young man sitting on a little pine tree, and he seemed to be alert, so I walked over and said, "Awahde," a Yiddish word that only someone who knows the language very, very well would know; it's colloquial for "sure enough." And—so the Germans wouldn't think I was speaking Yiddish—I said in German, "Er hat eine Wade entblößt," which means 'his knee is uncovered,' because it was the only thing I could think to say that had a word close to "Awahde" in it.

At this, the man understood and started to shake. Twenty-two people went with Rolf Peschel; three didn't want to. That's the first time I felt close to him. He took my hand, and I let him hold it. The first time he touched me, I felt like worms were crawling on my back.

After a few months, Rolf came to me and told me he loved me. "You're not even allowed to think of me," I said. I probably loved him already, too, because I was more concerned about his safety than my own. Germans were not permitted to socialize with Poles. And with Jews, it was *Rassenschande*—race degradation. "I don't care that you are Polish," he said. "It's worse than that," I answered, and burst out, "I'm Jewish." "Impossible! This is impossible!" he said. "What do you think?" I demanded. "A Jew has to be dirty? A Jew has to have horns on his head? I can't be a Jew because I don't smell bad?" At that point he ran away.

I was sure I was going to be arrested, but I had no more strength left to fight. I cried and cried, and just as I was falling asleep, I heard somebody on the stairs. I went to the door and opened it, and there was Rolf. He said, "I apologize for running away. I had to absorb it. It doesn't matter to me. I'm glad that I am a criminal police officer. I will watch over you, and you will be under my protection." He helped many Jews and Poles, more Poles than Jews, because my environment was Polish. Rolf later confessed to me that he was involved with the Polish underground.

Once we went to the theater, and when we came out, there were gunshots. We later found out that these shots were meant for us. The Gestapo had found out about Rolf and were after him. A few weeks later, in 1944, Rolf was shot and killed on Three Crosses Square. He was set up. Rolf had a new translator, a Nazi, and the Gestapo asked the translator to go with him to a camera store—photography was his hobby. "Take Rolf Peschel to the camera store," they said. "He is a traitor, we want to get rid of him." As it turned out, the Polish underground wanted to assassinate Rolf's translator. So they set him up. The translator left some film to be developed and said he would pick it up the next day at a certain time. The store owner called the underground, and the next day they were waiting, as were the Gestapo. So there was a shootout. In the end, both Rolf and the translator were dead. I will never know which side's bullets hit him. After Rolf was killed, I was in mourning. I mourned after him as I mourned after my husband.

In 1947 I came to America. Two years later I got married to an American Jew. Three years later I went back to Poland, and put advertisements in the newspapers, asking for information about my first husband, or my child, or his sister. . . . Nobody responded. I knew my husband hadn't survived, because he would have known where to find me. But throughout the war, I hoped that maybe he put the child somewhere with a Polish family—that what we had intended to do in Warsaw, he managed to do in Zlatov. Not only did I hope, but I think it was self-preservation; I could continue to hope the child was alive, or believe him dead and go insane.

I'm not defending myself, I'm accusing myself. I have always felt very strong guilt in me. Why is my righteous father dead? He was a good person. I'm not. And my child was innocent. What did he do to anyone? All these guilt feelings. When somebody gets sick, they say, "Why me?" We survivors also say, "Why me?"

I WAS LIVING IN VASCAUT in the province of Bukovina in 1941 when the Romanians came to our house. They took my husband, my little one-year-old baby, and me to the ghetto. That was only for a short time. What they really wanted was to make the town *Judenrein*–Jew-free–so they took us to the Dniester River. It took us three days to get there.

The soldiers made us give them our belongings, and they threw them into a ditch. It was December and very cold. I could see how cold my baby was. I talked with the others about what we should do. We couldn't stay there, we would die.

I went to the soldiers and asked them to help us. We gave them money and they gave us little boats to cross the Dniester. On the other side, we came to an almost abandoned village, Mogilev. Other Jews had already been settled there. We took a place in the corner of a ruined house and we slept. We were so tired.

A few days later, I heard a lot of noise, so I went out to see what was happening and I saw Romanian soldiers bringing other Jews– people from the concentration camp Yedenez. I knew my parents had been taken to this camp, so I waited and waited until my parents came. I told them to get out of the line they were in, but they were scared and wouldn't. I went to a Romanian soldier and bribed him, and he let my parents come back with me to our little ruin.

At 4:00 A.M. the soldiers told us we had to leave, that we had to go with them and march until we died. I told my mother that we were not going to go. So we went out into the garden and hid in a hole while they took all the people out of the ruined houses. We waited until there were no sounds before coming out of hiding.

We found a three-story house and stayed on the top floor so we could see when soldiers came. We were there over a month. There were 116 people hiding in Mogilev. We organized a committee and went to the mayor. He wouldn't let us stay in the area, but he said that in exchange for money, he would have some soldiers take us somewhere else. He suggested Djurin.

It was so cold. I asked the soldiers to let us build a fire and they said, "Why should we? You Jews should die anyway." So my husband and I got wood from the forest and made a fire. Many people died that night of cold and hunger. I remember one baby died; not mine.

We walked for four or five days before we finally got to Djurin. There was a collective farm outside the village with an open hangar. It was very cold. We had no food, no heat, no water, nothing. The soldiers told us if we left the area we would be shot by the Ukrainians. We had to sneak into the woods to get firewood. At night, we all slept close together for warmth.

The Ukrainian soldiers then told us we had to leave. We went to the village. Family and friends in Chernovtsy sent us clothes through a Romanian officer we bribed, which we could exchange for food at the market. We stayed with this one Jewish family for three years. As the Germans were leaving at the end of the war, they bombed the village, and my family and I went back to Chernovtsy.

"I SAW A CART CARRYING SUGAR BEETS TO A FACTORY. I GOT ONE BEET AND IT WAS SO GOOD, SO SWEET, THAT I FELT THE FIVE OF US COULD LIVE ON THIS ONE BEET."

MY SISTER EDITH and I remained together despite the many selections. Our secret device was to never show emotion and never give away that we were sisters, for the selection was severe, and the first objective was to break up families in order to make the fragile individuals more obedient. Only at night did we permit ourselves to whisper hopes to each other, to recall memories, to strengthen each other.

On Friday nights we tried to mark Shabbat in a special way. We played an imaginary game that we were at home. We talked about it slowly, recalling our home and Shabbat in minute details to make the picture firm and real. At home I always had the responsibility of setting the table, and mother would reprimand me if I forgot the smallest detail. In Auschwitz, these were precious memories, so our make-believe world would last longer and seem more real.

Edith would whisper, "It's time to set the table. Find the nicest tablecloths, and don't forget the flowers. Where are the napkins for the guests? You forgot the fork for Father. You really shined the candelabras beautifully this week, better than before," she added approvingly. After our imaginary meal, we would whisper the Shabbat songs, the *zmirot*.

Standing in line in front of the latrine, the twilight announced Shabbat. The stars, like whispering voices, ignited each other and covered the sky.

"Why don't we celebrate Shabbat with real *zmirot*, real singing inside the latrine?" whispered Edith.

"In the latrine?" I turned toward her in disbelief.

She nodded her head, her eyes measuring the distance of the SS guard. "This is the only place we are unobserved for a few minutes, the only place we are alone."

Far away, in a corner, we started our Shabbat songs. One by one, others gathered and joined in—recalling melodies, capturing memories. "Shalom aleichem, malachei ha-sharet, malachei elyon . . . peace be to you, ministering angels, messengers of the Most High."

From that time on, Shabbat was celebrated in the latrine of Auschwitz, and week after week more children gathered to join in—and the angels' shielding wings enveloped the voices and carried them beyond time and place. The inner light of Shabbat kindled a new hope for another day in Auschwitz.

"WE WERE MOSTLY CHILDREN IN OUR GROUP; WE HAD LITTLE IN COMMON, EXCEPT FEAR."

"THE CHINESE DIDN'T CARE THAT WE WERE JEWISH. AND THEY DIDN'T RESENT US. BASICALLY, WE WERE JUST AS POOR OR POORER THAN THEY WERE."

WE STARTED TRYING TO EMIGRATE from Berlin in 1937. Some relatives in the United States had gotten us affidavits, and we were registered for the quota. But the German quota was already so overcrowded that we had a few years wait until our number would come up. Kristallnacht was the final straw. My father decided it was time to leave. We would go anywhere.

We heard people were going to Shanghai. It was the only place you could go without a visa because it was under International Settlement Control. The British, French, and Americans all had fixed territorial rights in Shanghai. Another sector was occupied by the Japanese after the 1937 Sino-Japanese war.

There were only a few shipping lines that went to Shanghai. There was an Italian line that had three ships running from Trieste, there was a German line that went from Hamburg, and I think there were some Japanese ships. My mother stood in line for tickets every day for three months.

You had to list every item you were taking, down to the last sock. At the time we applied, you were still allowed to take valuables. Then, a month before we were ready to leave, they changed the law. All you could take was a wedding ring and a watch. And since the German government already had a list of your valuables, you had to turn everything in. I think we left with the equivalent of four dollars apiece. We had a big J stamped on our passports and the name Israel or Sarah added on.

Two years after the war started, Germany took away our citizenship altogether and we were stateless.

We took the *Contra Rosso* out of Trieste. It was a twenty-three-day cruise, made up mostly of Jewish passengers. Our route from Trieste was through the Adriatic down to the Suez Canal, stopping at Port Said, Aden, around the bottom to India, Colombo, Singapore, Bombay, then on to Hong Kong, and finally Shanghai.

We got to Shanghai on the seventh of May, one day after my fourteenth birthday. A committee made up of members of the local community and the American Jewish Joint Distribution Committee had been formed to take care of the arriving refugees. We were loaded onto trucks together with our luggage. Since several thousand people had already arrived, they had established what they called Hime—homes in camplike facilities in the Japanese area of Shanghai.

When we arrived, there was no housing available. So we were trucked to a synagogue not far from the waterfront. They put cots and mattresses and blankets on the floor. And that's where we spent our first few nights.

Then we moved into the Hima. My father and I were in a room with fifty other men, and my mother was in a room with fifty other women. We stayed there for the first few weeks. Eventually my father began working for a firm that canned eggs and exported them to England, and we moved out.

By the fall, a school had been established. The main benefactor was a man named Horace Kadoorie from an old established Jewish family that originated from Baghdad. There was a Shanghai Jewish Youth Association. We had meetings, outings, and dances. It was a thriving European-style community in miniature. There was theater. There was opera. It's amazing how people can adapt to the most adverse circumstances, and make do fairly well. We led a reasonably normal life. We had girlfriends. We had boyfriends. All within the community. We had no real social life with the Chinese.

We kept maps detailing the progress of the war. But we didn't know anything about the concentration camps. We didn't know what was going on in Germany. We had lost all contact. We had relatives there, but we never heard from them again. One cousin remained.

The day the Japanese bombed Pearl Harbor, I got up in the morning to clear skies and what I thought was thunder. What it was was the ships in the harbor being bombed and scuttled. The Japanese then rolled their tanks into the International Settlement.

In 1943 the Japanese issued an edict that all refugees—defined as anyone who arrived after 1938—had to move into a restricted area within Hongkeu, an area of about three-quarters of a square mile. This was essentially where most people lived anyway. But those who didn't had to trade their houses or businesses with people in the area, mostly Chinese or Japanese.

It was like a ghetto. There was no barbed wire, but there were posts with guards, some manned by refugees. You needed a pass to leave. If you were caught without a pass, you would be thrown into prison. I think the ghettoization was somewhat at the instigation of the Germans.

I didn't interact much with the Chinese, though more than most because I used to sell cigarettes. During the war people tried to buy things that would go up in value. You didn't keep money, because inflation was so bad. So people bought soap. People bought cigarettes.

I think I was probably the only foreigner who ever went to what was the Chinese equivalent of a commodities exchange for cigarettes. They traded in some back alley. I knew everybody, and they trusted me. Likewise, their word was as good as a written contract.

Then the bombing started. We had no basements. The only secure place in our area was the jail. There was a small room in a building next to where we lived, and we'd go there sometimes during a raid and sit with a washbasin over our heads in case the plaster fell.

During one raid I remember sitting there with this basin on my head and I could feel the air pressure from a bomb that was falling nearby. That was the one time the bombs fell in our area. Across the street was an antiaircraft battery and a Japanese barracks. People said the Japanese moved all industrial manufacturing into our area, knowing that the Americans wouldn't bomb us. But the hits weren't always accurate. That day about thirty refugees and several hundred Chinese were killed.

At the end of the war, there was an announcement on the radio. The Japanese emperor was talking. We heard something about a bomb. We didn't know what kind of a bomb it was. And then the second bomb was dropped on Nagasaki. And that's when we found out that the Japanese had surrendered.

The first Allied troops we saw were the Chinese. They had straw sandals. Then the Americans came. We got a collective affidavit sponsored by HIAS (Hebrew Immigrant Aid and Shelter Society) and came to the United States in 1947.

CONSCIENCE AND COURAGE | *by Eva Fogelman, Ph.D.*

INDIVIDUAL INSTANCES OF MORAL COURAGE during an immoral time–the period of the destruction of European Jewry–did not change the course of history. Nonetheless, the "righteous among the nations of the world"–in Hebrew those non-Jews known as Hasidei U'Mot Ha'Olam–are as much a part of that era's history as the gas chambers and ovens at Auschwitz-Birkenau. Not to record the altruistic deeds of ordinary men, women, and children (yes, children) is to deny that even in conditions of extreme terror people have a choice.

Seven hundred million bystanders looked on indifferently, and in many cases even approvingly, as Hitler directed the systematic murder of the Jews. The German directives were clear: the recompense for aiding a Jew in Poland was a death sentence. In other countries, the lack of a legally sanctioned death penalty did not prevent rescuers of Jews from being killed; the lucky ones were deported to concentration camps, only to confront death there.

With Nazi informers everywhere, eager to cash in on a pair of boots, a bottle of vodka, or five pounds of sugar for reporting Jews in hiding to the authorities, few bystanders were transformed into rescuers.

For bystanders with the ability to see through Nazi propaganda and the determination to act, "the hand of compassion was faster than the calculus of reason." At times, the jobs people held determined the kind of help they were able to offer. Doctors instinctively put up signs reading DO NOT ENTER, QUARANTINE when German Nazis or local collaborators were rounding up Jews from their hospital beds. German factory owner Oskar Schindler recruited Jews to work in an ammunition factory, insisting to the German authorities that these Jews were essential industrial workers critical to the German war effort. Raoul Wallenberg, Aristides de Sousa Mendes, and Sempo Sugihara, among other diplomats, availed themselves of their diplomatic posts to save thousands of Jews from deportation, provided Jews with passports as protected people of a neutral country, or gave them visas so they might flee to neutral territory. Nuns, priests, and teachers used their institutions and their professional roles to harbor children in their convents, monasteries, orphanages, and schools.

While many Christians turned their backs when Jewish friends knocked on their doors in the middle of the night, others, like the Western Ukrainian Zahajkewyczes, who lived across the street from Nazi headquarters, hid their Jewish neighbors in the cellar for a night and then built an extra shelf in their pantry for the couple to sleep on. Janny Blom, a dental hygienist in Amsterdam, begged her old Jewish boss and his wife to move into her spare room, lest they be deported with the other Dutch Jews.

To endanger one's life for an old friend is understandable, but how to explain such action for total strangers? Looking back in some instances, rescuers' behavior was not understandable even to themselves. How could they have endangered their families? How could they have given up the comforts of home and lived like nomads, transporting people across borders to foreign lands?

I at once sympathize with and am irritated by an unfathomable mystery. Clearly human behavior is complex, inconsistent, and changeable. Reason doesn't always prevail. So much of how rescuers reacted depended on singular combinations of circumstances, personalities, feelings, and personal history, crystallized into a single moment.

Unconscious motivations certainly played a role in turning a bystander into a rescuer. Yet intangibles such as personal gratification and enhanced self-image were small rewards indeed for the vast risks these people undertook.

My empirical research and analysis has begun to show that there were clear social and psychological motivations beyond the unconscious. Rescuers saw people who were different from themselves and responded to the imminent threat to those people; they responded not to differences, but to similarities. While most bystanders saw Jews as pariahs, rescuers saw Jews as human beings. This humanitarian response sprang from a core of firmly held inner values, which included, among others, an unwavering and immutable acceptance of people who were different. And central to these beliefs was the conviction that what an individual did, or failed to do, mattered. They recognized that the choice they made could mean life or death for a Jew.

Motivations were complex. In relationships between rescuers and Jews that stretched into four and five years, motivations changed. What began as an altruistic deed of saving a baby became a chance to have a child of one's own. What started out as an opportunistic relationship to acquire material possessions from Jews turned into an occasion to be selfless when the money ran out. Ultimately, it is the survivor as witness who can attest to the subtlety of this complicated relationship.

The rescuers of Jews during the Nazi occupation look like a haphazard collection of individuals–aristocrats and poor farmers and shoemakers, educated professionals and illiterate semiskilled workers, avid religious believers and antireligious Communists and socialists. But surprisingly, they share similar humanistic values. It was not mere whim that led these people to risk their lives and those of their families, but a response—almost a reflexive reaction in some cases—that came from core values developed and instilled in them during childhood.

Interviews with rescuers left me with no doubt that the experiences and values inculcated in them at an early age had an impact on their ability to stand up to racism and to empathize with those persecuted. Many rescuers attributed their strength to their parents' love and nurturing. But what I found as well was an altruistic parent or beloved caretaker who served as a model for altruistic behavior and engaged the child in helping others; a tolerance for people who were different; a childhood illness or personal loss that tested resilience; an upbringing that emphasized independence, discipline with explanations (rather than physical punishment or withdrawal of love), and caring.

Of course, not all rescuers experienced one or more of these factors, but a majority did. Nor were their childhood influences sufficient by themselves to transform them into rescuers. The circumstances, timing, and contingency for responsibility were necessary ingredients in the alchemy of their transformation.

In the words of Hannah Senesh, a Hungarian poet and emissary from Palestine who was tortured to death by the Nazis for parachuting behind enemy lines and attempting to free other Jews, the importance of the rescuers resonates:

There are people whose brilliance continues to light
the world though they are no longer among the living.
These lights are particularly bright when the night
is dark. They light the way for Mankind.

Eva Fogelman, Ph.D., is author of *Conscience and Courage: Rescuers of Jews during the Holocaust*, coeditor of *Children during the Nazi Reign: Psychological Perspective of the Interview Process*, and writer and coproducer of *Breaking the Silence: The Generation after the Holocaust*. Dr. Fogelman is a social psychologist, psychotherapist, filmmaker, and founding director of the Jewish Foundation for Christian Rescuers, ADL.

L E I F D O N D E | *Born* 1937 | *Birthplace* Copenhagen, Denmark | Refugee in Sweden

Occupation Former United Nations ambassador from Denmark | *Current residence*

Buenos Aires, Argentina

I WAS THREE YEARS OLD when Denmark was overrun by the Germans in 1940. My first recollections of the German occupation stem from around 1941, when I started kindergarten. I remember being told by my mother that when walking to the kindergarten together with my older sister, never to talk to the German soldiers in the street. Seeing soldiers with green uniforms and black leather boots, I knew that they were the enemy.

I remember that blackout curtains had to be drawn every evening to avoid air bombardments by the Allied forces, and seeing the night skies aflame in red and yellow colors from the ever-increasing sabotage activities of the resistance movement and the retaliatory bombing by the Nazis. I also recall numerous times being woken up in the middle of the night by the shrill sound of air raid sirens, and being rushed down by my parents into the shelters of the basement.

My most vivid and exact early recollection dates back to a Saturday visit in 1943 to the famous Tivoli Garden amusement park in the center of Copenhagen. Coming out of the park early in the evening, we saw a large convoy of armored German trucks and tanks rolling through the streets.

Later on, I was able to pinpoint the exact date: it was August 28, the day the Danish government decided to step down, refusing any further cooperation with the German forces, who immediately declared a state of emergency and martial law.

I recall my dad coming home early one day in September 1943, asking us all to dress warmly and prepare to leave the house within half an hour. My two siblings and I were told that it was dangerous to stay at home, since the Germans were looking for us. The family therefore had to spend the night at the house of some friends. To remain inconspicuous, we were told not to take any luggage.

My father had tried to secure passage to Sweden from the north of Copenhagen, where the sound separating the two countries was at its narrowest point and could be crossed under normal circumstances in less than half an hour. But his efforts had proved unsuccessful, and the following day we took the train to the southern part of Denmark.

On the train, I suddenly caught sight of my uncle and aunt, but was immediately told to pretend not to recognize them. It was important not to draw attention of any kind, since the German soldiers were riding the same train.

Two nights later, after a drive through a dark village and forest—there was a curfew on and no street or road lights were allowed—we reached a deserted beach. The only sound was the light engine noise of an approaching fishing boat. While waiting on the beach for the boat to dock, I remember that my dad, who was a chain smoker, started to light up a cigar. I warned him that the light might attract the Germans. He put the cigar back in his pocket, and of course I got praised for being so attentive. We finally boarded the fishing boat, and embarked on an eleven-hour, rather dramatic journey.

It was a small, very old fishing boat, certainly not meant for the transportation of human beings. There were seventeen of us on board. We were placed in the hold beneath the deck. The stench from the fish was terrible.

The boat was handled by a couple of young men, nineteen and twenty-one years old, who had no previous experience running a boat. One hour out to sea, German patrol boats detected us and started to give chase. The young skippers, hoping and assuming that the boat had a sufficiently shallow draft, decided to run the risk of entering the minefields. Fortunately, their assumption was correct, and the Germans stopped their pursuit. The weather turned rough—we were awfully sick—and twice the engine failed.

The next morning, we finally reached a small port. As soon as we entered the harbor, however, the sight of green uniformed military men on the pier combined with the knowledge of the inexperience of the skippers caused much despair on board. There was fear that we had arrived in Sassnitz on the German coast of the Baltic Sea instead of Sweden. But much to everyone's relief, the soldiers were Swedish, and it turned out that we were in the southern Swedish port of Trelleborg.

Two hours after we landed in Sweden, the old fishing boat sank in the harbor. But we were lucky. We were safe. We were among more than seven thousand Jews who, in a matter of days, were illegally sailed to safety in Sweden as part of a spontaneous and improvised rebellion against the inhumanities brought upon Denmark by the occupation.

I have often heard it said that it would be understandable and justifiable if the Danes were to feel a little proud of the success of the September 1943 events. But Danes in general do not think back upon these events as reflecting any kind of outstanding national achievement. Rather, they think of them as natural joint efforts to help fellow human beings in distress and great danger.

Danes do not in any way consider the rescue operations as heroic acts. As a Dane, I certainly understand this attitude, but as a member of a Jewish family, I count myself very fortunate and privileged indeed, that in September 1943 we lived in Denmark.

HERTA: I was born in Vienna, Austria, on October 7, 1923, as Herta Wellisch, the older of two children. My father worked for the Austrian government. We had a good life. There was always anti-Semitism, but you learned to ignore it somewhat. At the same time, you never told somebody right away that you were Jewish.

Life was good until Hitler marched into Vienna in 1938. Chancellor Schusnig said that he wanted to avoid war between brothers, so he was going to abdicate to the Nazis. The next day they were there. And right away on most houses big flags with swastikas were flown. Very soon after that, my father was dismissed from his job at the railroad because he was a Jew.

WILLIAM: The Nazis showed up in Vienna on March 12, my mother's birthday. I was twenty-six years old and in charge of a department at a factory. When I came to work the next day I was immediately discharged. In July 1938 my two younger brothers and I went by train to Freiburg, Germany, through the Black Forest to the German border. We crossed the German border illegally and entered Switzerland.

HERTA: Otto Preminger had arranged for my mother's sister and her husband to go to England. My uncle, who was one of the best tailors in Vienna, had made costumes for Preminger's films. I went to join them as part of the Children's Transport. I left Vienna on August 9, 1939, just three weeks before the war. I was very lucky. That transport was one of the last.

The morning after we arrived in London, I had such an unreal feeling. I wasn't even sure if I was alive. I became a maid in training with a wonderful childless couple called the Baileys. They lived in a little town near Edinburgh. Early the following year my stay with them came to an end because the English were afraid of fifth column activity. Anybody from an Axis country who lived in a coastal area had to be evacuated. My foster parents tried desperately to keep me, but to no avail.

Around that time I got a letter from a refugee organization called Bloomsbury House, where I had applied for a job. They told me about a magical place called Susua, in the Dominican Republic, where I could go and even potentially bring my parents and brother. I didn't ask any more questions, I just filled out the form.

WILLIAM: In 1940, an agent from the Jewish Federation who represented the Dominican Republic came to speak to us and told us that the Dominican Republic was the only country in the world that, at the Conference of Evian, had agreed to take at least a hundred thousand Jews. President Trujillo had even set aside land on the north coast specifically for that purpose. Whatever supplies would be needed, he said could be imported from the United States duty-free. The only requirement was that we had to agree to become farmers.

HERTA: On our approach to the Dominican Republic, it looked very beautiful. Very lush, very green. There was a big mountain. I think it was called Isabella. Forty or so people were already in Susua when we arrived. There had been one previous transport directly from Germany. We went through customs and boarded a big truck to Susua.

WILLIAM: I arrived in Susua very early in 1940–January, I think. They had built quite a few barracks, where all the men and some of the married couples stayed. The single girls all lived in a two-story house. We had a community kitchen, but we had no idea how to prepare the food. We finally learned from the islanders. I still like certain foods we learned to eat there, like roasted yucca, yams, and plantains, and lemonicas, which look like green cherries.

HERTA: Life in the Dominican Republic was so entirely different from anything we had known. We weren't used to the subtropical climate or the sand fleas. But of course we felt we were the lucky ones because we had a life. Susua was a real Jewish settlement.

The wonderful thing about it was that when the Dominicans said, "Ah, you are a Jew from Susua," they didn't mean it as a derogatory statement. They said it with very high esteem. Today, you can see a lot of kids of mixed marriages walking around with big Stars of David and yarmulkes because they are so proud of their Jewish heritage.

Meanwhile the war was raging, and more and more bad reports came from Europe. Most of the young people I came with were in the same situation I was in. They had family in Vienna or in Germany and hoped to get them out. We were worried from one letter to the next that our parents might be deported, and many were. I was very lucky. I was able to send my parents a visa.

Very soon after I had sent my parents their visa, my husband-to-be came to Susua. We saw each other in the barrack where we ate. I remember he was sitting next to a young woman, and I was sitting next to a young man. There was a table between us and when we saw each other, we both thought, "What a pity that this person is married." I was seventeen at the time. We met a few days afterward and hit it off very well. We got married in July 1941.

We had to go to Santo Domingo to the cathedral to get married because that's where the justice of peace was. There was no synagogue yet in those days. But that didn't matter to us. We just wanted to get married. We've been married fifty-four years.

'AFTER A FEW DAYS, WE KNEW EVERYTHING. WE SAW THE FLAMES GOING UP TO THE SKY. WE KNEW THE FIRES WERE BURNING A LIGHT TO GOD, WE THOUGHT MAYBE GOD WOULD DO SOMETHING."

~HARRY JOSEPH FELDINGER

I WAS BORN IN MUNKACH IN 1931. It was Czechoslovakia at the time. Before the war, there were about 25,000 Jews in Munkach. My father's name was Shlomo. My mother's name was Shlime. My Jewish name was Cheske. We were an average Orthodox Jewish family. We were a family of nine—my father and mother, four sisters, and three brothers. I was the first boy after three girls. I was king. Out of the three boys, only I survived. And out of my sisters, only two survived. I was in my fourteenth year when I was taken away from home.

The Germans were very systematic. When they went into a city, the first thing they did was take all males between the ages of eighteen and fifty-five to forced labor camps. So the only people left in the city were children, women, and older people. Then they ordered all the Jews to move into a designated number of streets—a ghetto area.

On the day the Germans came, the Hungarian soldiers chased everybody out of their houses and rounded them up in the middle of the street. I remember my sister telling my mother, "I forgot to lock the doors," and my mother saying, "Don't worry about it. We're never coming back here again." We didn't.

We were loaded on cattle cars—jammed full—and shipped to Auschwitz. No one knew where we were going, just that we were going to be resettled in Poland. When we arrived at Auschwitz, my sisters and my younger brother went with my mother. That was the last time I saw them. I went with my father.

They marched us to a barrack where they cut off our hair. Then they gave us showers. We were able to keep our shoes. Everything else we had to leave. When we came out of the showers we got our prison clothes—pants, a shirt, a jacket, a cap, no underwear. Then we were led into one of the sections. We were fed once a day, ten people to one bowl of soup.

One day they told all the young boys that we would be getting different food. They told us to go into the barracks. So we did. I don't recall how many we were—twenty or thirty boys. They locked the barracks from the outside while they took our fathers to be killed. That was the saddest day of my life. If G-d didn't hear the screams of those children . . . it's very tough to believe in G-d, very tough. I might wear a yarmulke, but I find it very difficult to believe in G-d.

When they opened the doors, my father was gone. And I became a different person. I grew up. Instead of a fourteen-year-old kid I became a twenty-four- or thirty-four-year-old man. Survival was the game.

At first I was assigned to cleaning the grounds of the camp, or the section I was in. Later, after a while, I was moved to the shit commando. We were eighteen or twenty boys, and we cleaned out the sewers of the camps, going from section to section every day.

That's more or less how life went until around the end of September 1944. Then they began the selections of young people, presided over by, I assume, [Josef] Mengele. If you passed the selection you went about your routine again until the next selection. The Nazis chose Jewish holidays for their selections. In the second selection, you had to hold a pole and he [Mengele] knocked it with a stick; whoever couldn't hold the pole straight was sent to the gas chamber. Life then went on again for a few days or a few weeks, until they decided to kill us all.

We were on our way to the gas chambers when I just walked away. The guard was right there. And all I thought was that G-d blinded him, that finally G-d blinded him and he didn't see me walking away. I walked behind the barracks to barrack 7, and I told one of the men there that I was going to hide in the oven. I asked him to please lock me in and to come and let me out when *Appel*, counting, was over.

The Germans were very precise. When they took people out of camp, they knew exactly how many were taken. You had to be dead or alive. You had to be accounted for. This time, when they counted, there was one person missing, and that person was me. So they started screaming at the barrack commander to check the barrack to see whether someone was hiding, or lying dead. There were two little holes in the oven, and he heard me breathing. He opened up the oven, saw me, and closed it again. I thought an angel from heaven had come to help me. But it wasn't to be. It wasn't long before a couple of German soldiers came and dragged me out. They hit me over the head with a whip and took me to the front of the camp. One soldier took my head between his legs and put me on a stool and two other soldiers beat me, but after two or three it could have been a hundred and two, it wouldn't have made a difference.

When they finished beating me, they threw me aside, and I was dragged to a barrack where they put people who were sick or old, people who were to be disposed of. The Nazis would collect them all in one barrack and then during the night take them away by trucks to the gas chambers. When they threw me into that barrack, I knew right away that I was doomed. I couldn't sit or lie down because of the beating that I got, so I stood while one of the guards walked back and forth with a stick, warning people not to escape—not that you could anyway, since the barrack was locked from outside. I watched him go back and forth, estimating how long it took him to walk from one end of the barrack to the other.

After timing him for quite a while, I knew I would be able to

"ONE THING MY FATHER TOLD ME BEFORE WE WERE SEPARATED, 'DON'T FORGET WHERE YOU COME FROM. WHEN ALL THIS IS OVER, GO HOME.' THOSE FEW WORDS ARE THE ONLY REASON I SURVIVED."

climb on top of the oven when he was walking in the other direction, and from there to the top of the beams, then jump out of the window and off the roof, run across to the latrines, and let myself into the latrine without being caught.

But I had to belong to a barrack. I didn't have my numbers yet. Everybody had a little piece of a rag on their lapels stating which barrack they belonged to. So early the next morning, I pulled a rag off someone's lapel. I noticed I belonged to barrack 24.

Then they selected people again, and all the young people were taken. It was during Sukkoth (Tabernacles). This time, there was no escape. They told us to undress. There were numbers on the walls so that we would remember where we hung our clothes, they said. We stood in line for the gas chamber, about a thousand people. But all of a sudden the SS came in and started hollering, "Alle Jugend auf eine Seite!" which means, "All young people on one side." Kids like me—thirteen-, fourteen-, fifteen-year-olds. They selected about fifty altogether and took us to the D section—the working lager. And then they tattooed my number on me. My number was B14670.

Very early one morning, 3:00 or 4:00 in January 1945, we were liquidated, marched toward Katowice, Poland. At some point I fell down and just remained lying there in the snow. I woke up about an hour before daybreak and looked around. Everybody was gone. There were dead people lying all over the roads. But I kept walking until I walked into a little town. I went into a general store, wearing my clothes from camp, and my number, which was in a red triangle with a yellow stripe. The yellow stripe meant I was a Jew. The man in the store probably knew that, and he pulled out a gun and chased me into the road, where someone turned me over to the Gestapo. I was fourteen.

The Gestapo took me just outside of town together with other stragglers like myself. They lined us up in the square in a half-circle and set up a machine gun. We were all veterans of Auschwitz, so naturally we knew what that meant. But just then there was a big bombardment, and while everyone ran for cover I escaped.

Eventually, I was caught again and sent to Mauthausen. When they opened up the wagons, people ran to the bread car, and as they did, they were shot. They cut our hair, like a mohawk, in the middle. We were given another number, on our wrists. After our showers, we were chased out naked in the freezing cold of the winter, and we had to stand outside until the following day when they brought our clothes back. Half the people dropped dead. How I survived, I couldn't tell you. But there had to be survivors. And I was a survivor. Like my father told me, I had to go home.

THE TRANSPORTS TO Theresienstadt began in 1941. I and some other young people were called in May 1942. We were allowed only a certain amount of luggage. I think it was the equivalent of fifty pounds. I remember taking along a mathematics book of my father's that I figured, for the weight, would give me the longest entertainment. They marched us through the streets of Prague to a fairground where they were collecting everybody.

When we arrived at Theresienstadt, I realized it was not necessarily the ultimate destination. I was sitting there reading this strange book when a young man came by and asked me, "Would it be okay with you if I told the officials that you are my fiancée?" I was a little befuddled by this and went to ask my mother what to do. She was much brighter in this respect and she said, "Of course." It turns out this man belonged to the original group that came to the camp–called *Aufbau*–and they had certain privileges. They were allowed to protect two people each. I stayed this young engineer's fiancée until October 1942, when some real relatives of his came to Theresienstadt.

I worked in an office in the technical department. People were hungry, not starving but hungry, and yet there was an amazing amount of cultural activity. In general, life was bearable. We were idiotically optimistic that it would soon be over. But, of course, it was terrible whenever they collected people for the transports, because by then we knew what was going on. I remember the famous Red Cross visit. It was so frustrating, because all of us would have loved to somehow get our message across.

In October 1944, when my mother and I were called for the transport, I couldn't find a way out. And so we went by way of the famous cattle cars to Auschwitz. I felt very fatalistic, but somehow stepped outside of myself and looked at it all like a distant observer. I guess it was self-preservation.

In Auschwitz came that terrible moment when my mother went to one side and I to the other. Not that I knew what it meant. But somehow, you got the feeling of doom. The whole trip prepared you for this.

Of course, the usual horrors occurred. They shaved our heads. They took everything, although there wasn't much left. We only stayed in Auschwitz for a week. Looking back, I can't understand how people lived in Auschwitz more than a month. I mean, people stayed there years, and how they survived even half this, I don't know.

We went on to a place called Urderon near Kemlitz, which was not far from Dresden. It was a work camp, a former textile plant turned munitions factory. The local people working alongside us constantly asked what we had done to be in this prisoner situation.

After the Battle of the Bulge, the Germans started to get nervous. They evacuated us; I think they wanted to take us to Buchenwald, but they couldn't get there anymore because some of the railroad tracks had been destroyed. So the train was eventually routed back to Theresienstadt. We had a horrible trip. There was no food, hardly any water. We stole turnips wherever we found them. It was April when I returned to Theresienstadt.

Then the rumors about the Germans planning to blow up the camp began circulating. There were also rumors that the Russians had arrived, then that there was a train going to Prague. So five of us walked to the train station. Nobody stopped us. There was so much disorder. . . . We just got on the train and went to Prague.

Amazingly, I had very little wish for revenge after the war. I mean, not that I had the chance to do anything, but revenge was not the driving force for me. And this puzzles me, because there are many of us like this. The only parallel I found is with the Japanese, who also did not have feelings of revenge after the camps here in the United States. I don't know what would happen if I were face to face with the labor camp overseer or Mengele, but when I meet young Germans I have absolutely no negative feelings.

"EVEN WITH REGARD TO MY MOTHER'S KILLING AT AUSCHWITZ I FELT DEEP SORROW, BUT NEVER RAGE. THIS IS UNUSUAL FOR ME BECAUSE I DO HAVE A TEMPER."

WHEN I WAS ABOUT TWO YEARS OLD, my parents moved from Vienna to Chernovtsy, a province of Bukovina that belonged to Romania. They rented a little room. And in that room lived my parents, me, and at least one grandmother and a cousin. Somehow we found that room enough, and nobody got in anybody else's way.

In Chernovtsy, there were mostly Jews but also Ukrainians, Romanians, Germans. And we all spoke each other's languages and sang one another's songs. We were good neighbors.

I got married in February 1941 to a cousin of mine. The Russians came that same year, after the Hitler-Stalin pact, and right away they arrested some ten thousand people from our city. My father had a fabric store and he was arrested as an antisocialist, which he wasn't, and sent to Siberia. He never came back.

When the war started, my husband and I were not in Chernovtsy but in a little village on the River Dniester that formed the border of Poland and Romania. My husband was a young doctor and sent by the Russians to work in the provinces.

It was summertime, and my mother and little brother came for a visit. On June 22, 1941, the Germans invaded Russia and the Russian soldiers ran away. There was no resistance.

My husband was recruited to minister to some villages, so my mother and brother and I were left alone. We saw the Russians retreating, and I said to one of the soldiers, "Take us with you. We will be left here for the Germans." He told me, "Don't worry," and walked away, smiling.

When my husband came back, together with another doctor and his family, we decided to leave. We crossed the Dniester into Poland.

We stayed in a little village overnight. The Jews there said, "You're going with the Russians? Do you know how bad it is there? Stay here." But we figured it was still better with the Russians than with the Germans. So we continued until we came to the village of Borshev, in Hungary.

Almost everybody had left. The Hungarians were allied with Hitler. We found an empty house and moved in. We had nothing to eat or drink, but my mother was a person of initiative. She walked from house to house asking for food. And she came to one house that belonged to a Gottesman. It seems he was the leader of the community and a relative of ours.

He advised us to go back since when the Germans came, we would be the first to hang because they will say we deserted with the Russians.

When we got to the Dniester, it was raining, and the bridge was broken and we couldn't pass over it. My mother had some relatives on this side of the border, so we stayed there overnight. The next day, my husband, my brother, and I climbed over the broken bridge and across the Dniester. When we came to our house, everything was missing.

Later that afternoon some Romanian soldiers appeared. My husband ran and hid in the outhouse. My twelve-year-old brother jumped out the window. But they caught him and brought him back in. They asked me, "Where's your husband?" I told them he had gone to see a patient. They had come to tell us that we had to report to the main building the next morning at ten o'clock. We could bring with us a package that weighed up to ten kilos.

I went to sleep. A terrible rainstorm erupted; since we were on the Dniester, there was heavy flooding. Suddenly everything was resolved, I didn't have to worry anymore. The next day, the Romanians couldn't carry out their plans because of the rain.

They told us to get ready, that the entire Jewish population was going to spend the winter on a farm. Nobody thought that people would be shot. The fact is that people were shot in all the villages. In some, families were tied together with barbed wire and sent to the river and shot there. A few of these families managed to escape, and they went to the town of Zastavna to report what was done to them. They had no idea that the order had come from high up. So the policemen took them back and did the same thing.

Finally, we bribed our way back to Chernovtsy. Our house happened to be in the ghetto. So everybody we knew came to live with us. But then they started the deportations to Trans-Dniestria, which was actually the Ukraine, on the other side of the river Dniester, and where we had just come from. Some 80,000 people were deported from Chernovtsy; 10,000 came back.

People were killed by the peasants or by the soldiers. In our village, they didn't do us any harm. But in Babin, in Kisselev, in the other villages, all the Jews were killed.

Anyone who remained in the ghetto had to have authorization to stay. A relative of ours got two sets of authorization papers, so he gave us one. One day everybody had to have their authorization papers checked. My husband was afraid to go, so I went. The official looked at the document, then looked at me, and said, "You're trembling. Are you scared?" After he gave me back the papers, he said, "You were scared." He recognized that something in those papers was fabricated. But he didn't say anything. Pretty soon they started taking you even with authorizations. Every month or so there was another transport.

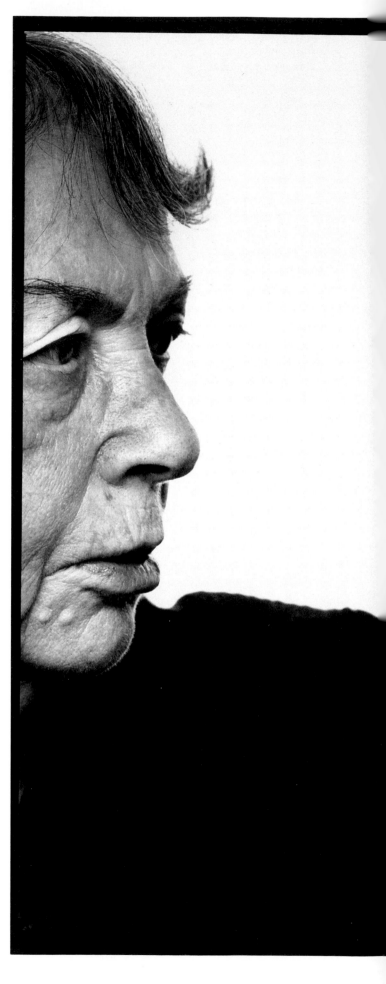

"WHEN THEY TOLD US WE HAD TO REPORT THE NEXT DAY AT 10 O'CLOCK, I KNEW SOMETHING VERY BAD WAS GOING TO HAPPEN AND I PRAYED TO GOD THAT THE WORLD SHOULD GO UNDER. THE WHOLE WORLD."

We used to send packages to people who were transported to Trans-Dniestria. If somebody let us know they were still alive, we sent a package.

Finally a miracle happened–the Yalta Conference. The Allies and Stalin made a pact to free the people from the Romanian provinces occupied by Russia. The ghetto was dissolved in 1945. They opened the gate and everybody was allowed to move back to their houses. We still had to wear a yellow star, and there were still restrictions and deportations, but we were able to go to Bucharest, where we stayed until 1947. From there, we went to Vienna. My husband became chief doctor in the displaced persons camp. We came to America in 1951.

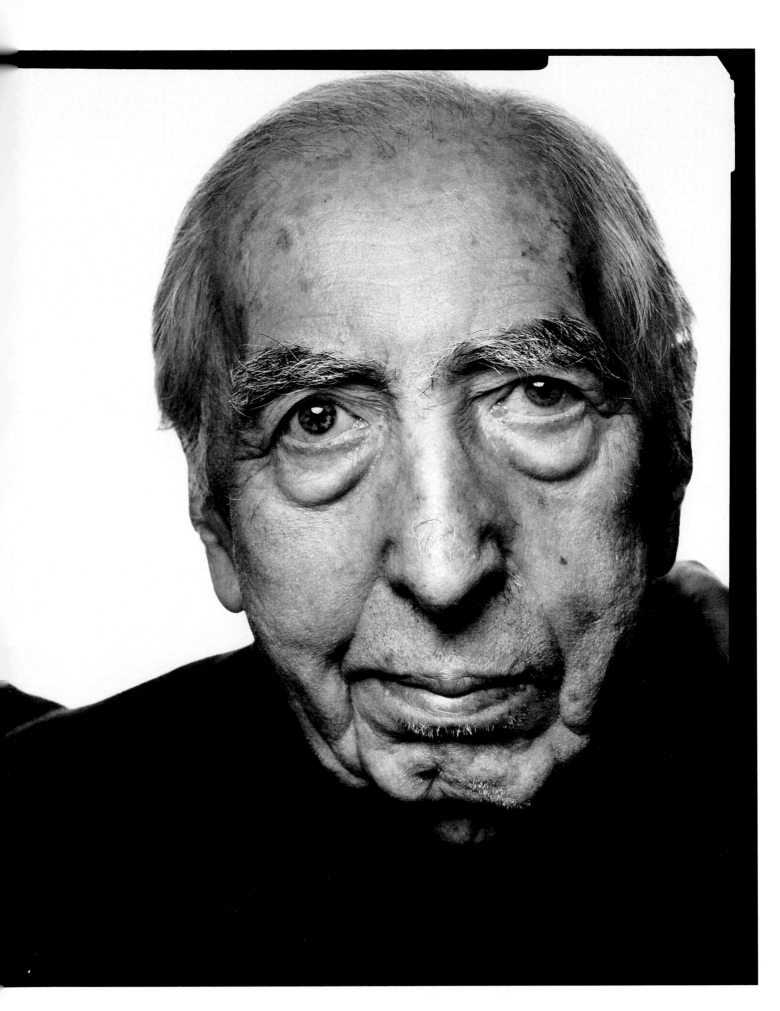

WOMAN: There was a Greek song the EEE, the fascist organization, used to sing by my house:

Na zisi o Kosmidis mas
Na zizi, na yerasi
Kai sta makria moustakia tou
Evarious na kremasi
Sti souvla na perasi
Long live our leader Kosmidis,
May he live to an old age,
May he hang the Jews from his long moustache,
May he skewer them on a spit.

MAN: They took us to different camps from the age of seventeen or eighteen. I worked in a camp that was a limestone mine at Asvestohori, near Salonika, for six or eight months. But I got to go home at night to sleep. I was deported in April 1943. There were three or four transports before us.

MAN: I used to go to hear the chief rabbi, Tzvi Koretz, talk at the Beth Shaul synagogue. One time, he told us we should get good shoes, heavy coats. "You are going to work," he said. "It's going to be light work. They [the Germans] will give you food; they will give you anything you want."

WOMAN: We trusted Koretz because he was our chief rabbi. Who else are you going to trust?

WOMAN: They used to take us in sections, small sections at a time; seven, eight thousand people.

WOMAN: The chief rabbi didn't come to the concentration camp with us.

MAN: Some young people in Salonika managed to escape. They went to the mountains. And that demanded a certain degree of sacrifice on their part because they had to leave their parents behind.

WOMAN: We got off the train at Auschwitz and the selection began. We were separated from our families right away. In the morning we saw the flames and the smoke and we asked the other people in the camp, "What is this?" They answered, "Your parents."

WOMAN: They took us to the showers and cut our hair. We didn't recognize each other.

WOMAN: I didn't even recognize my sister!

WOMAN: I was very lucky. The block supervisor loved my voice. She took me by the hand to every block to sing. I used to sing "Mamma, son tanto felice." They went crazy over that song. It had just come out in Greece. We were so depressed, singing that song.

We cried, because we knew we didn't have mothers anymore.

MAN: Then there came a request for musicians. I used to play the trombone. Friends of mine had just arrived from Salonika and they said, "Why don't you go try out?" I was weak and said that I couldn't play. But they took me over there and said, Jacob is a musician. So they gave me a piece of music to play and they kept me there. Of the 400 people in the orchestra, there were only about 50 Jews. The other 350 were German and Austrian political prisoners.

Being a musician in Auschwitz was a different life. I stayed in a different barrack together with the rest of the orchestra. Every Thursday they used to give us an extra piece of salami. I used to play in the morning and in the afternoon when new transports arrived, before they took them to the showers. We stood by the gate that said, ARBEIT MACHT FREI, work makes you free. We also used to entertain the Germans. They split our orchestra into different groups, and we would play in different barracks.

WOMAN: The orchestra played while people burned.

MAN: They took five hundred of us to work in Warsaw. I found thirty men and women, hidden, still alive. They couldn't speak. The Germans killed them all and told us to put logs on them . . .

MAN: Our job was to tear down the ghetto houses. We were in Warsaw almost a year. We built a camp there. It was filled with two thousand Hungarian Jews who came with their suitcases directly from their homes.

WOMAN: We were working in Kanada commando when we saw the crematorium in Birkenau being blown up. The women who worked in the munitions factory used to collect gunpowder every day, little by little, and sneak it over to the men.

WOMAN: These two Greek brothers, Saltiel and Dario Venezia, who worked at the crematorium, planned to blow it up. The wife of one of these brothers was with us in Kanada. When she saw her husband singing the Greek national anthem and jumping into the flames, she ran toward him; the Germans shot her. Up until that point, she hadn't even been in contact with her husband.

WOMAN: The women who brought the gunpowder to the men were caught and hung in front of us. We had *Appel*, and then they gave us a piece of bread.

MAN: We stayed in Auschwitz until January 1945, when they started evacuating the camp. It was nighttime, stormy weather, snow. We walked all night. If someone fell down, the Germans shot him in the head. Then they put us on open trains and transported us to Germany. From there we were sent to different work camps. We ended up in Dachau, near Munich. But that didn't last long. As the Allies were advancing, the Germans didn't want to leave us there. Obviously we were evidence of something. They took us to the Ural Mountains. The American and British air force started shooting at the trains. They didn't know who was inside.

They stopped the train, and in the morning we saw the American army tanks. I was very sick by then. I had typhus. There was an American sergeant, a Jew, whose parents happened to be from Greece. He put me in a hospital and came to see me every day. They rebuilt me.

I wanted to go back to Greece to see who was still alive. So from Germany, we went to Bari, Italy. One day, some Greek Jews came from a different camp in Italy, and they had a list of people in that camp who were going to Palestine. My oldest brother was on this list. So I contacted him and we both went back to Greece. From the whole family, only the two of us survived.

MAN: The Israeli Jews were so angry at all the Jews from Europe. They said, "How could you let yourselves be picked up like that in animal cars? Why didn't you fight? Why didn't you rebel?" How could we fight? Nobody had with what to fight. We couldn't do anything.

WOMAN: We were so degraded.

WOMAN: The Jews in the Warsaw ghetto fought. What happened? They were killed.

WOMAN: My husband and I were in Kaufering together. I saw him, and he was gorgeous, but I couldn't do a thing except look at him across the barbed wire. We got married afterward in Germany in a displaced persons camp. The Americans had opened these offices, and they had mass weddings! We went back to Greece, to Salonika, where we stayed five years.

We had parties every night. We only wanted to live and have fun because we knew everything was gone, and we had to continue living. But we also knew that this was going to be with us all our lives. We made history. And we knew it would happen again. It is happening again in Bosnia. We had nightmares for years; we have nightmares now—again we're going; again they're taking us.

MAN: My grandfather was born in Jerusalem, my father was born in Yugoslavia, my mother in Bulgaria. I was born in Greece, my wife in Germany, my son in Israel, and my daughter in America. This is what it is to be a Jew.

IN AUGUST 1939 MY HUSBAND, Fred, went to London on business; he imported and exported grains. On September 1, the Germans invaded Poland. His friends in England said, "Don't go back. Have your wife come here." But he came back to Rotterdam and said, "If we have to fight, I'll fight." On May 9, 1940, my husband's family left for America via Belgium. We took them to the train and said good-bye. Three hours later my husband woke me up and said, "I'm afraid we are at war." We lived very close to a river, and we saw the German planes and parachutists coming down. The first thing my husband did was take all material that could be death for us if found, letters, books, down to the cellar and burn it all.

After five days of tough fighting, the heart of Rotterdam was bombed severely until it became a city in flames. Only then did Holland surrender. Many Jews committed suicide. We felt that we always would be able to do that should worse come to worst.

The first year or so, we went on with our lives. In Rotterdam it was less severe than in Amsterdam. Amsterdam had a ghetto; Rotterdam didn't. There were fewer Jews living there. In August 1942 my daughter Dorien was born, and we were all very optimistic, we thought the war wouldn't last long; many Jewish people were having children around that time. Then one day we had to wear Jewish stars, we couldn't use public transportation, we weren't allowed to have a telephone or radio or buy in regular stores. The rounding up of Jews had begun.

Non-Jewish friends took care of us. On April 9, 1943, our neighbor upstairs got information that we were on the list to be picked up that evening. So other neighbors took us in at great risk to themselves. The next morning, since our apartment wasn't sealed, we went back. We had the opportunity to put Dorien in a convent. But when we could not be assured that she wouldn't be converted, we said no. In the meantime, the firm where Fred was a vice president came under German control, and he was forced out.

Then on September 29, 1943–the night before the eve of Rosh Hashanah–two German SS and one Dutch Nazi came to our door at midnight; we were on the list, but my daughter wasn't. Dorien was thirteen months old. We didn't know what to do. So we took her with us to German headquarters.

When we got to headquarters, there were all our friends; this was the last roundup of the Jews in Holland. My husband talked to the commandant of the German unit and asked if he could leave Dorien with some gentile women who had accompanied some old Jewish women to headquarters since she wasn't on the list. He said, "I wouldn't advise you to do that." And then he turned around, and said, "Well, if you want to, go ahead." Maybe he had a little girl Dorien's age, or a grandchild. . . .

Fred gave these women the address of our friends who would take care of Dorien, and we left her there in her stroller and went to the bus. I didn't say anything. I let my husband make all the decisions. Just before the bus left he ran out to have one more look at her. There she sat screaming at the top of her lungs, surrounded by SS. Fred picked her up and took her and put her on my lap. It was the best thing he ever could have done. Without Dorien, probably none of us would have survived.

We were sent to Westerbork, a Dutch concentration camp and transit camp for deportation to Poland. It was like a vacation compared to the other camps. We were assigned certain tasks, but mothers with children under three years old didn't have to work. And that saved us. I didn't need very much food, so I could give the food to my husband, who I felt needed much more.

Monday nights, though, were terrible. Tuesday the train would come to take two thousand people to Auschwitz. We didn't really know anything about Auschwitz–we thought there were labor camps where you would have to work hard, but we didn't know anything more. Monday night they would read the list of the people who had to go. And it was always a terrible moment. We had received from my husband's relatives in Mexico papers to go to Palestine (where a limited number of people were allowed to go, in exchange for German POWs), so we were never on that list, but many of our friends were. After the train left, life went on as if nothing had happened, until the next Monday night.

We were sent to Bergen-Belsen in February. We didn't know much about it except that it was an exchange camp. People with papers for Palestine would be exchanged for German POWs in England. We were supposed to be in the second group of exchanges, but by that time, no more exchanges were taking place.

It was okay at first. You had your own bed, and the beds were next to each other, not on top of each other, not yet. And there were, I think, only 250 people in one barrack. When we came to Bergen-Belsen, the camp held about 4,000 people; when we left in April 1945, there were 70,000.

In the fall of 1944 Bergen-Belsen was declared a concentration camp. By that time we were given one piece of bread a day and one pint of water that contained turnips and potato peels. Hunger became the enemy. I saw men sneaking around when their wives and children were asleep to steal their bread rations. To fight the hunger, people started to give lectures; the women exchanged recipes.

"THE FIRST WORD MY DAUGHTER DORIEN SPOKE WAS 'ACHTUNG.'"

In the last phase we had beds three bunks high. And there were people on top who couldn't climb down anymore; if they had to go out to the outhouse, it was awful . . . diarrhea all over. You tried to keep clean, but there was only cold water. We always said, "It can't get any worse." And it always got worse, until the end.

As time went on, my mother got weaker. I probably did too, but I always said, I can't get sick—the first day we are out of here, then I will be sick. In January 1945 my mother said to me, "Well, I can count on my five fingers how many more days I will live." She was in the old-age barrack, everybody was dying. I said, "No way. We came here together and we get out of here together. You're not allowed to die." She didn't.

There were wonderful times, too. There was the sunset, the heather, and you could see so far that you forgot you were in this place and couldn't get out. In the summer of 1944, Dorien started to walk by herself and speak full sentences. It was remarkable that notwithstanding these extraordinary circumstances, most children seemed to develop normally.

One Hannukah, we had a musical afternoon. A woman from Rotterdam sang Ave Maria, and every time I hear it now, I start crying. It was wonderful, absolutely wonderful. So there were times when we laughed a lot, when we were just mothers and children in a small barrack together.

My faith became much stronger, really. I was very impressed by the Orthodox people in the concentration camp—how they behaved, how they kept holy days—it impressed me tremendously. There were Passover seders two years in a row. People stood watch outside so the Germans would not come in and surprise us. Matzoh was made from flour and water, obtained secretly from the kitchen. People were all around the table or on their beds listening to the reading of the Haggadah. We understood what it meant to be slaves, and G-d would save us from our enemies. History had become reality.

On April 9, 1945, we were sent east to Theresienstadt. I knew that many people who went to Auschwitz went through Theresienstadt. We had known about Auschwitz since the beginning of 1945, maybe the end of 1944, because we got barracks from the east. And there were messages scribbled on the walls. And butterflies . . .

We were on the train for two weeks. Every day there were new corpses to be buried. Sometimes there wasn't even time to do that. We went through Berlin, then east to Leipzig and Troebitz. On the morning of April 23, we woke up and the Germans were gone. We were among very few Dutch Jews who returned.

TO LIGHT DAILY SIX MILLION MEMORIAL CANDLES | *by Yaffa Eliach*

IT IS A PRIVILEGE TO BE A JEW in the twentieth century. It is a miracle to be a Holocaust survivor. It is a miracle that carries with it great obligation and the responsibility to light daily six million memorial candles, so that the memory of the victims and their vanished world will burn forever like an eternal flame, a pillar of light. To assure that the dark night of the Holocaust will never return. To assure that the Jewish identity of the victims be preserved and the landscape of death of the mass graves, ghettos, and death camps be guarded against reclamation by the various nations as their exclusive national and religious sacred grounds. We must assure that the uniqueness of the Holocaust be understood and its lessons incorporated into the history of mankind.

As a hidden child, I see it as both a privilege and an urgent duty to document the Holocaust and the vanished world of the martyrs with accuracy, dignity, love, and sensitivity, and to teach it to future generations. In 1970, I was among the three individuals who initiated Holocaust studies on the Brooklyn College campus. In 1974 I founded the Center for Holocaust Studies Documentation and Research.

The center's goal, and that of my own research, is to rescue victims from their anonymity and restore their human dignity. The "Tower of Life" in the United States Holocaust Memorial Museum is a tribute to the victims' dynamic, creative lives prior to the Holocaust.

The commitment to this project was made in August 1979, on a plane between Warsaw and Kiev. I was in the middle of a fact-finding tour to Eastern Europe as a member of President Carter's Holocaust Commission. Our charge was to recommend to the president an appropriate memorial to the Holocaust, to be built in Washington, D.C.

During my travels to Warsaw, Treblinka, Auschwitz-Birkenau, Plaszow, and other capitals of the Holocaust kingdom, I was struck by the fact that a thousand years of vibrant Jewish life in Poland were being reduced to mere images of victimization and death. Now, as we flew over Vilna on our way to Kiev, I was aware that somewhere beneath the clouds was the shtetl of Ejszyszki, home to the early years of my brief, interrupted childhood. One of the oldest Jewish settlements in Lithuania, Ejszyszki was founded in 1065. Among its first five Jewish settlers were my paternal ancestors.

Then and there on the plane I decided to create my own Holocaust memorial, in the form of a written history of Ejszyszki. Rather than focusing on the forces of destruction as most memorials do, it would commemorate every aspect of the long life of the community. And though I did not then know what artifacts I would find for such a collection, I committed myself to gathering together everything I could find from the shtetl. As one of only twenty-nine survivors, I wanted to memorialize as many of its former inhabitants as possible, both those who left and the 3,500 who remained in the shtetl—who were murdered on September 25 and 26, 1941, by the Einsatzgruppen (the German mobile killing squads) and their Lithuanian collaborators.

The first photos, the foundation of my shtetl collection, were from my brother Yitzhak. As the collection grew, so did my familiarity with the history of each person in the photos. Behind every peaceful image lurked a tragic tale of death and destruction.

In 1987 I returned for the first time to Ejszyszki-Eishyshok-Eisiskes. As I stood on the mass grave, which was covered with green grass and yellow buttercups, I was riveted to the place. I could hear the voices of the thousands buried beneath my feet. I had read their letters and diaries, collected their birth and marriage certificates, pored over their family records; my neighbors, asking with new urgency to be remembered.

Soon afterward, back in the United States, I met with several people from the United States Holocaust Memorial Museum, among them Ralph Applebaum and Cindy Miller, who were searching for a way to commemorate the one and a half million Jews who had been murdered by the Einsatzgruppen. Sitting at my kitchen table, they looked at a small sampling of my collection. A few days later Ralph, the exhibition designer, invited me to view something extraordinary in his SoHo studio: the model of a tower that he envisioned as home to 1,500 of my photographs.

In April 1993 the United States Holocaust Memorial Museum in Washington, D.C., opened to the public. Since then the "Tower of Life" has become the virtual symbol of the museum, singled out by many as the museum's most moving exhibit.

At the museum opening, I stood in the middle of the tower surrounded by photos of most of the shtetl's 3,500 victims, including my murdered family, my gentle mother, and my energetic grandmother, Alte Katz, the shtetl's leading photographer for thirty-six years. I firmly held on to my beloved grandchildren with their bright faces, sparkling eyes, and sound Jewish education. At that moment I knew that Hitler had lost the war, and we who survived the Holocaust had won.

But the time is short, and there is yet much work to be done, for the life and death of the majority of the six million exist only as lost ashes, evaporated smoke, and mass graves. There are still many candles to be lit.

Yaffa Eliach is a Broeklundian Professor of History and Literature at Brooklyn College.

I'LL NEVER FORGET KRISTALLNACHT—November 10, 1938. I was a young boy at the time; I had just turned fourteen. I was on my way to see a friend. I didn't know . . . I just didn't know . . . I saw the stores smashed in with axes, shattered glass from the windows everywhere. People were being dragged out of their stores and beaten up and trampled upon. There were trucks on the streets collecting Jews. They took them all to a central place where people stood around beating them with sticks, screaming, "Dirty Jews! We should kill you all." All the schools and community centers were filled with people, and you could hear the screams from the beatings; you could hear the Viennese people saying, "Let's burn down all the Jews." People who had Jewish friends, who worked for Jews, who went together to the coffeehouses, who played football together, all of a sudden they changed completely. They were not the same people anymore.

There wasn't one corner that wasn't in flames. The city was in shambles. They went wild, running after people wherever they could. Everyone tried to get off the streets. The SS started to call people to see if they were home. But nobody would answer their telephone. People knew . . .

My grandfather had a beautiful shul on Baurelegasse—Bais Yitzchok—which was about forty years old. It was rectangular in shape, with two long tables against each wall and rows of benches across. The people who belonged to the synagogue were very devoted to my grandfather; many knew him from Poland.

On Kristallnacht, the Germans came and took out all the religious books and three or four of the Torahs—we were lucky, one part of the Ark was closed, so the other three Torahs were spared. But they took out whatever they saw and burned it. They burned the shul, all the chairs, everything, completely. My grandfather was devastated. I was devastated, too. Of course, I was too young to comprehend the real tragedy.

The Nazis started going from house to house to pick people up. They came to us, too. Two SS men came barging into our apartment on Klosterneubergerstrasse. The one in charge pushed everything away and turned over all the furniture. He said to my father, "You come with us." My mother started crying, screaming, "What do you want from him? He didn't do anything." "Er muss gehen"—he has to come with us—he said. My mother tried to tear my father out of the SS officer's grip, and he punched her in the stomach. But she didn't let go. So he hit her again, and she had to let go because the pain was too great. He said, "You dirty Jews, we're going to kill you all anyway sooner or later." The other man wanted to take me, too, but the one in charge told him to leave me alone.

We didn't know what to do. My mother tried to find out where my father was. We knew they put him in jail, but we didn't know where. Finally an SS officer told my mother, "We're going to send him to concentration camp." We had no idea what that was.

The Germans put everyone on wagons; they had guns, little revolvers. My father had to stand looking into a sharp light. The SS man kept making the light stronger and stronger.

When they got to Dachau they had to stand in one place for three days without food. They couldn't even use the toilet. After three days the Nazis put them in barracks. But for a week and a half they didn't let them sleep—all night they woke them up. And in the morning, they had to march just the same. All day long they had to march. This was in the middle of winter, in November. And every day they took out someone else from the barracks and tied him to a tree and left him there. That was their sport.

My mother and brother and I remained in Vienna. My mother couldn't do too much, but she did what she could, trying to get information about my father. We were at the police station a week after Kristallnacht when they told us my father had been sent away, to Dachau probably. We didn't even know what that meant. We started asking questions, but people came with whips, chasing us away. After that, I didn't dare go out. We had curfews. I couldn't go to school anymore. I think I went out twice. We just stayed home and waited. And we started making arrangements to leave.

We were lucky. My father came home soon. He was back in Vienna about two weeks before Christmas. My mother had a cousin in Switzerland who knew somebody who was friends with Himmler. He and another cousin paid this man about 10,000 Swiss francs for my father's freedom. When my father walked through the door, it was terrible. He looked like a corpse. He was very sick. He couldn't sleep; he was shaking and screaming all night. For two years, he continued to shake and scream.

Our family in Switzerland arranged for us to get out of Vienna. We got a visa to Mauritzia and a transit visa allowing us to pass through Switzerland. But once we got to Switzerland, we stayed.

I'm not afraid the way I used to be. But a little bit of fright is with me all the time. I'm not completely free of fear. The hatred of Jews is very great, and it gets greater every day.

A lot of people lost their faith because of the Holocaust. I didn't. I'm still alive. I was protected by G-d in a way. I cannot speak for those who were killed. . . . We just have to believe.

"WHEN THEY CAME TO TAKE MY FATHER, IT WAS THE FEAR OF THE UNKNOWN. WOULD HE EVER BE BACK AGAIN?"

~ADOLF HAGER

"THE MENGELE TWINS BECAME THE MOST EXCLUSIVE CLUB IN THE WORLD."

~IRENE HIZME

MY FATHER WAS FROM Germany and my mother from Russia. But René and I were born in Czechoslavakia. All I remember about my dad being taken from us is this man coming into our apartment. There was a lot of arguing, crying, and screaming. We only learned in the last few years that he was sent to Auschwitz. At some point after my father was taken, my mother and René and I were sent to Theresienstadt. I can't say I was scared. I sensed my mother was nervous and scared, but I didn't know what was going on. We were four years old.

My memories of Theresienstadt are kaleidoscopic. I remember a very long train ride, waiting in line for food, cobblestone roads and dead bodies on carts. And then one day, I guess it was the day we were being shipped to Auschwitz, I remember a very long walk to the train. There were a lot of people, it was snowing, there were dogs barking, and I heard the sound of rifle fire. I remember holding onto my mother's hand. I was always holding onto her hand.

We were with our mother for the first four months at Auschwitz, and then one day I guess they decided we were old enough to do without her, and we were separated. Actually, the entire *lager* was terminated. I think the only ones who survived were a few sets of twins. I remember it was very, very still, and there was all this sobbing.

When it came time for them to take my mom, she didn't want to let go of us, and we didn't want to let go of her. We heard this horrible screaming and one of the guards just hit her and she fell to the ground. And we never saw her again.

René and I were separated. Siblings of the opposite sex didn't get to stay together. As part of Mengele's great scientific plan to find a master race, he had a passion for studying twins. Usually one twin was the control and one was experimented on. It seemed I was the lucky one who got to go to the hospital for all kinds of experiments.

Could I pick Mengele out? Never in a million years. I only remember a doctor in a white coat. He once gave me candy. It was all so innocent. He was our savior and our demon. You had this ambivalent feeling, wanting him to like you. I would think, I'll be really good and then he'll be my friend, then he won't hurt me. But it wasn't like that. There are things that I've never spoken about, that I don't think I'll ever be able to speak about.

I remember having a lot of blood taken from me, from my neck. It was so painful. I got injections, and I would be very sick afterward. But all of us children were very good. We knew instinctively that we had to be. There was no such thing as having blood taken and crying. You didn't dare cry. Very early on I remember being worried about René because he was such a crybaby. I was

scared that he was going to cry and something horrible would happen to him. In a way, maybe it was better that I was the one experimented on because I was more of a stoic.

I remember once hiding among dead bodies. I knew that these were dead bodies, but to me, it was what you had to do. I could see the chimneys day and night. I knew something terrible was going on. But I figured when my turn comes, it will be my turn.

It's very hard to really find the right words to explain what I felt as a child. I lost my childhood, I had no childhood. I remember having a doll that René smashed. Unbelievably, that was a real memory, even in the camps. But if I'd still had her then, I wouldn't have known what to do with her anymore. I remember thinking, who is in charge of this place? Is G–d in charge of Auschwitz?

I was so scared all the time. And I felt so alone. One night I had to go to the bathroom and then tried to come back inside. It was dark and I got confused and didn't know where my bed was. I was groping, trying to find my way back, and people were pushing me away. "This is not your place," they said; grown people pushing me away. I felt so rejected, I can't even explain it. Finally, somebody said, "Okay, you can stay with me for the night."

Toward the end, I was so sick and weak that I just lay on the ground for days wondering what was going to happen. Finally a Polish woman picked me up and took me to her house. It was a mixed blessing. The American Jewish Joint Distribution Committee came to get me. I was almost eight years old.

After that, it was one orphanage after another until I was adopted by a wonderful family in Long Island, and from the moment they found out I had a brother, they spared no expense trying to find him. René meanwhile was in Czechoslovakia. We finally got him out in 1950.

Sometimes people ask, did it make you a stronger person? I don't know. I don't think suffering makes you strong. It made me a lot sadder. There's always something missing for me…in everything. There are times I feel like I'm three years old and I just miss my mother and father, and I wish I could have known what they were like.

After the war, nobody wanted to hear what happened. At the time, there was no real help, no community to turn to. The thought was, you're here in America, be American, fit in. So I learned to fit in. I fit in so well, you'd never know what was going on inside of me. I was the best student, I won all the awards, I made the speech at my graduation. I fit in great. But I didn't. Every day, there was a shadow. Even now, I try not to think about it, but there isn't a day that I don't get sucked into this big black hole.

I WAS BORN IN ITALY, but my parents were Czech. They lived in Italy because my father had tuberculosis as a young man and he needed the warm Italian climate. Unfortunately my father died when I was two years old.

And so my mother was left alone in Italy. My mother was a pianist and a writer. She wrote for travel magazines. At the time, I think Mussolini was already in power, and it was dangerous to be in Italy, or so one thought. So my mother took me to southern France, and we lived in Nice for a few years. In 1943 the Germans came to Nice and my mother placed me in a convent. I was about seven years old. It was the last time I saw my mother.

I recall arriving at this place that was very isolated, just outside of Nice. It was in the hills beyond the harbor and overlooked the Mediterranean Sea. It was a convent of cloistered nuns. They were able to hide children because Nice was the center of the underground. The archbishop of Nice, Msgr. Raymond, a wonderful man, arranged for us to stay there together with some Christian children. But the irony was that just across the street there was this huge hotel that the Germans had requisitioned. And very often a German priest would come and give Mass, with all the kids there in the dorm. The presence of the Germans was always so close.

I recall this small room with iron grids and a huge woman who was dressed in what seemed to me an absolutely bizarre brown outfit with a hood. There was this white thing around her face and her cheeks puffed out because of it. I almost laughed. She introduced herself as Mother and said that the woman with her was Sister so and so. I was so confused.

I was told, either by the nuns or my mother, that my mother would come back for me in a week. And of course she never did. This was the first time I was really lied to. Then they told me that she was in Corsica, that they were writing letters to her from me. There was this huge charade going on. Of course, what else were they going to do?

I remember being in this garden and looking up at the roof and seeing the nuns walking around the roof and praying. They never looked down at me; I always looked up, hoping that they would look at me. I felt so alone. My mother had been very affectionate, and I missed that affection; I couldn't understand why they ignored me. Later I found out it was a sin for them to look at people. They were supposed to only look at G–d.

I was converted. Water was poured over my head, and I was given the name Flora Marie. I didn't so much mind being con-

verted because I liked the rosary. We used to play this game, seeing who could go faster during prayer. I remember, too, Christ on the wall in the dining room, where there was total silence. It was spooky. But what really got to me was the story of the Jews killing Christ. I knew I was Jewish, and somehow I started to feel that I was implicated in something I knew nothing about.

The day we left, I remember somebody telling me that my name now was Flora Marie and I was born in Corsica. My mother had embroidered my name on all my clothes, and they proceeded to rip all the embroidery off. I still remember, it was almost as if they had finished me, wiped out my identity. I threw a terrible tantrum. And of course they got very upset because that was all they needed, a screaming child. I never really forgave them that. I lost not only my identity, I lost everything. I knew then that I'd never find my mother again. Somehow I felt it.

We were all packed into a truck in the middle of the night. At some point the truck stopped, and I was placed on the road. And this woman took me in. After that, I went to many different places. For me, the most traumatic thing about the war was being told I had to leave with no explanation. Everything was always so sudden. There was no time to get ready for anything. There was never any time to say good-bye. . . . At one point, I was taken to Grasse, and placed on a bench in the square. All these people were arguing about how they didn't want a child. All of a sudden I was this hot potato that nobody wanted because it had gotten to be too dangerous. And I think I just became like a blank wall, totally shutting out my feelings.

Then this old man approached me and asked if I wanted a piece of sugar. His wife came up and they told me to come with them. We walked for hours. I had blisters on my feet. They lived between Grasse and Cannes. It was like the end of the world. He was a Protestant, from Sweden, and she had been Jewish but was now a Buddhist. She always made me feel, from the beginning, that she treasured me. Their names were Andrée and Aalrich Hogman. We had a close call with the French gendarmes, who were looking for Jewish children, so I spent the last several months of the war there locked in a room.

After the war I was converted to Protestantism. So I grew up Protestant, with a Buddhist influence. I was so envious of my friends at school, all of whom were Catholic. Here I was, this Protestant girl who wanted to be Catholic. And in the end . . .

I led a double life. I thought I was Andrée's daughter. I think

"I THINK I SHUT OFF ALL UNDERSTANDING. THE ONLY THING I KNEW WAS THAT MY MOTHER WASN'T THERE. AND I KNEW I WASN'T SUPPOSED TO SAY I WAS A JEW. IN SOME WAY I GUESS I KNEW I WASN'T SUPPOSED TO EXIST."

~FLORA HOGNER

I was working at Scandinavian Airlines at the time, and one day I saw this tall American come in; his name meant nothing to me. It took me fifteen minutes to realize he was my cousin. I almost fainted.

Later on, I discovered some relatives in Israel who told me that part of the family had tried to get me back after the war and my adoptive mother never told me. I was so angry, because I had felt like I was on this earth with nothing.

As for my mother, I found out years later that she was on the list of people who had been deported to Auschwitz. I knew she'd been taken to Drancy in France, but for years I thought that she was alive someplace in Russia.

Six years ago I went back to the convent and had a very emotional encounter with the Mother Superior who was a novice during the time I was there. I told her why I'd come, and she remembered me. "I remember your name," she said. "We could never look at you, but we always listened." And, apparently, prayed for us too. I was so shocked. Because I had had an image of these women who were just totally indifferent. It had never occurred to me that they were praying for us.

For years, I didn't want to discuss the past. The only reason I have started talking about it is because I felt a part of me was missing. I've become a specialist in a way. I'm the first person who wrote about the coping mechanism of hidden children, the positive aspect of trauma, new identity and trauma. That's not what I wanted to be known for. But I had to integrate those parts of my past for my own sanity. I had to try and unearth those memories by writing, and by going back.

I'm glad I found a way to begin to put things together, but I'm angry that I had to do it, that I had no choice. I've started to somehow come to terms a little bit with my identity conflicts, and with being Jewish and trying to like it. All I knew about Judaism was that I was almost killed for being a Jew. So for me, being a Jew was a very negative thing. My adoptive mother couldn't stand Orthodox Judaism. So I had total contempt for Judaism in general. I've been trying to go back to my Jewish roots. But I'm still somewhat conflicted. It's still difficult for me to say I'm a Jew.

I don't have any children. And about that I'm very sad. I think part of the reason is I never knew what I wanted to be. I've always asked myself, with all I've gone through, will I light the candles Friday night? Then everybody would have to know I'm a Jew, I'd have to acknowledge it. And I'd be terrified.

Andrée, and at the same time I was still waiting for my mother to come back. I thought for years that she was in Corsica like I had been told. I kept this sense of distance from the war, believing that somehow all these things happened in another place, another time. I grew up thirty miles from the convent, and yet it never occurred to me to go there. It was like a world that I knew of but could not touch.

And so it was the same with my mother. For years I prayed for her to come back. And at the same time I had gotten very attached to my adoptive mother—she was like a mother to me. I was with the Hogmans until they died. She died when I was eighteen, and he died when I was twenty. And then I came to the United States.

When Andrée and Aalrich died, I sent a letter to everybody in their notebook. One of those addresses belonged to my father's sister and her husband here in America. So one of my cousins came to Europe to find me and bring me back.

MY MOTHER SURVIVED the pogroms in the Ukraine during the Communist Revolution in 1917. In 1921 she and her parents succeeded in getting into Poland, where they were told that if they went to Cuba they might stand a better chance of getting into the United States. My mother got married there, and I was born in Havana. I was an only child. My parents went to Brussels in 1929. They were Orthodox, and although I attended secular schools, all my friends were Jewish. I belonged to Zionist youth organizations like B'nai Akiva, a religious group, and subsequently to Gordonia. By and large, the Jewish population, the great majority of whom were recent immigrants from Eastern Europe, kept to itself.

In the mid-thirties Jewish refugees started arriving, first from Germany and then from Austria. Most people in Belgium did not have the foresight, and of course couldn't conceive of the tragedy that would happen. Jewish people in Belgium said, "Well, Hitler is not going to come here," although there was an active Nazi movement called the Rexistes headed by Degrelle—an evil omen of things to come. Had we known what was going to happen, we would have sold everything and attempted to flee to Cuba or some other haven.

I will never forget Friday, May 10, 1940. We were awakened by the roar of planes. Hitler had invaded the Lowlands. A lot of people tried to flee. My dad and I tried to escape, too. The roads were clogged with masses of people, and the Germans raided these columns of refugees with Stukas. Ultimately the German army caught up with us about fifty miles from Dunkirk, and we went back to Brussels.

There was a progressive deterioration of the situation. One of Hitler's first measures was the forced registration of Jews. Everybody had to carry an identity card with a picture. Jewish identity cards were stamped with a big J–*Jude*. Then Jewish-owned businesses had to put up a sign identifying themselves as Jewish enterprises. Finally, Jews were forbidden to own businesses altogether. In 1942 Jews were expelled from school.

In June 1942 Hitler issued a decree that all the Jewish young people had to go to an assembly place to be sent away for work. Hitler worked through the *Judenrat*, the Jewish Council, to cajole the Jews—particularly the young Jews—to go voluntarily for labor, with the promise that if they went, their parents would be spared. So many thousands of young people went in order to save their parents. But eventually, of course, we got the complete message. No sooner were these youngsters sent out than they disappeared.

The younger people—particularly those who belonged to the youth movements, like Gordonia—assisted by the Belgian underground, organized an underground railroad to Switzerland. We got false identity papers, and a number of youngsters made their way illegally to Switzerland. But by and large, there was very little systematic organization of activities along these lines. This was the extent of our 'underground.' But in a sense it was a resistance, because we didn't just go voluntarily.

We were in hiding with a woman whose daughter, Rachel, was my girlfriend. Her father had been taken to a concentration camp earlier. In October of 1942 we made our way to Switzerland with false papers. A smuggler led us through the woods. He took us to a certain point, then told us where to go, after which we were on our own. Imagine a field that is lit by the moon and in one spot, a watchtower. We had to cross that field to get into Switzerland. Suffice it to say that we succeeded in crossing the border and were sheltered overnight in a farm. The next morning, we tried to make our way to Bern. Unbeknownst to us, the clerk who sold us our train tickets notified the Swiss gendarmerie, and they picked us up on the train. They took us back to the border and said, "If you come back, we'll hand you over to the Gestapo." The Swiss sent back one hundred thousand Jews.

The Nazis enlisted the help of someone we called Jacques the Musser, the denouncer. He was a Jew who went to work for the Gestapo. He rode around in Gestapo vehicles and helped them pick up Jews. He sent his own family to death. He was the one who picked me up.

I was brought to Gestapo headquarters in Brussels, and from there transported to Maline, an assembly camp. My father intervened with the Swiss consulate, and because I was a Cuban citizen, I received a *Schutzbrief*—a letter of protection—and was released.

On November 6, 1943, I was again picked up by the Gestapo, only this time with my father. On January 14, 1944, my father was sent with the twenty-third transport from Maline. On January 17 he was gassed and killed. My father's attitude was most remarkable. He was an Orthodox man, and his faith never wavered, even under the most trying circumstances.

In February 1944, because I was a Cuban citizen, the Nazis sent me—together with a handful of people who were either English or American—to internment camp number 194 in Vittel, in eastern France. Our camp was liberated by the Second Armored Division on September 2, 1944. I was reunited with my

'FOR EACH JEW THAT WAS DENOUNCED, PEOPLE GOT FIFTY FRANCS; FIFTY FRANCS AT THAT TIME WAS ONE DOLLAR. A JEW WAS WORTH ONE DOLLAR."

mother, who had been hidden in a hospital, in November 1944.

I always felt and still feel very strongly that real punishment was never meted out to the Nazis for the unspeakable crimes they committed. You can try to rationalize it any way you want, but the bad people were not punished. One example: Leon Degrelle, the founder and head of the French-speaking Nazis in Belgium, fled to Spain. He's still living there; Spain refused to extradite him. He is one of many.

I think that what the world did to us is unforgivable. I don't have much confidence in people. That doesn't mean I don't have confidence in friends or family. I do. But people at large, nothing that happens would surprise me. Because what happened to us was the most extreme, most hateful thing that humans could possibly do to each other, short of a nuclear holocaust.

~ISAAC JARKOVSKY

~FROM LEFT, MAX JUKERS WITH HIS BROTHERS, SOL AND SIGMUND

"AFTER THE WAR, WE WENT OUT INTO THE STREETS OF THE CITY AND COULDN'T BELIEVE WHAT WE SAW.

THE GERMANS CAME INTO CZARNOW on a Friday morning. It was such a black day. For three days and three nights, we watched the German soldiers come with trucks and tanks. They had the name of every Jew in our town. We couldn't hide. We couldn't escape. I decided to go to the Russian zone to check it out for the rest of my family. But when I got there, I couldn't get back. So I went to a little town and worked in a bakery.

Then some friends and I decided to go back across the border. It was lucky for me that I left that day. I found out later that one thousand Jews had been taken out of the town I was in and shot the exact day I left.

When I got back to Czarnow, I had to hide in my cousin's house under a hole in the floor. The Gestapo were looking for anyone returning from the Russian zone and would kill them if they found them.

I ended up in a labor camp called Baltroup South, not far from Auschwitz. Our job was to take apart houses that belonged to Polish peasants and rebuild them for German officers.

Sometime in 1943, I was sent to another camp, Kletendorf, which is where my brothers and I met up again. My brother Sol came through on another transport in June 1943.

My sister had arrived at the camp earlier. The *Judenaltester*, the head of the Jewish Kapos [prisoners who were foremen of labor squads], fell in love with her, and they were married in the camp. At the time, my brother Max was in a different camp. My sister found out which one and, through her connections, got him transported to our camp. By the time Max got to the camp, he was about 80 percent dead.

Our job was loading steel onto railroad cars from six in the morning to seven at night. We worked hard so that we would not get transported to Auschwitz. We never knew what happened to our parents.

SO MANY DEAD BODIES, IN THE WATER, EVERYWHERE. I HAD TO CARRY MY HORSE ON MY BACK; HE REFUSED TO GO BECAUSE OF ALL THE DEAD BODIES."

WHEN THE WAR BROKE OUT, I was a young boy of fourteen, fifteen years and when it ended, I was twenty. I lost my entire family. When the Germans entered Sassow in 1941, they gave the Ukrainians a free day to kill the Jews, to make a pogrom. My brother was one of the first. He was brutally murdered by a Ukrainian school friend. My father and I carried him to the cemetery and buried him. And then the trouble started. By the end of 1942 the Jews of Sassow were evacuated to another bigger city—Zlotchow—where there was a ghetto. In March 1943 the ghetto was liquidated. That was when I lost my parents and my sister.

They brought people by truck to twelve big graves that had been dug before. They all had to undress and stand on wooden planks. Then they were machine-gunned to death on the edge of those graves. The rivers of blood ran all the way down for weeks. And the ground was shaking for days because a lot of people weren't completely dead. They didn't even use bullets for the very small children. They just took the babies by the legs, hit their heads against the trees, and threw them in.

I was taken to a concentration camp in Sassow, where I stayed until a Friday in July 1943, when our camp was surrounded by German soldiers and Ukrainian and Lithuanian police. It was liquidation day. They had come to kill us. We were about five or six hundred young people, and we started to organize ourselves, to put up a resistance. We wanted to break through the gate; at first, there were only twenty or thirty armed soldiers. But then the Germans saw what was happening, and within minutes came hundreds of Germans, and then it was all over.

They surrounded us and started taking us one by one by one to be shot. One young man, Yaakov Pluchenik, stood guard and yelled to us, "Hurrah Yidden, toit oder leiben Am Yisrael chai!" Hurrah Jews, dead or alive, long live the Jewish people! He immediately received several hundred bullets. A friend sitting next to me yelled, "Run for your life!" They blew his head off. And we started to run.

Next to the camp, there were very deep woods and forests that stretched for hundreds of miles, all the way to Kiev, without any roads. Somehow around forty of us broke through the gate of the camp and escaped. Everyone who remained was shot. They poured gasoline over them and burned down the whole camp until there was nothing left.

We had been preparing ourselves for this moment; we knew the day was coming because everything was being liquidated around us. While we were at the camp we worked in the mountains, making rocks into little stones that could be used to build roads. Somehow, we had bribed the German in charge, and every day a group of us went into the surrounding forests and dug hiding places for the entire camp. We had weapons there and everything. We had all decided to leave on Monday, and they came Friday. If they had come three days later, nobody would have been there and everyone would have remained alive.

A group of us, five boys, had bought hand grenades. We wanted to hide them in the camp in case the Germans came before we left. But two boys insisted on telling the commander of the camp, who was Jewish, that we wanted to bring grenades in. The commander warned us that if we did, he would denounce us to the Germans and we would all be shot. As it turned out, this commander was the first one shot.

We had to run a whole day through rivers and around in circles because we were afraid the Germans would be able to track us. Finally, we got to the place we had prepared. Just about a mile away was another bunker of eighteen people. The two people on guard there were very tired after a whole day of running, and they fell asleep. While they slept, the Ukrainians came with machine guns and killed all eighteen people. They escaped from the Germans, and the Ukrainians killed them.

In my group there were about fifteen or sixteen people. After those eighteen were killed, we made sure that nothing would happen to anyone else, because there were a lot of Jews hiding in different parts of the forest. One day, we found out that someone had gone into a village to get food and was killed. So our leader went into that little village and burnt the whole place to the ground. Whenever we found out that someone had done something to a Jew, we killed the person, we burned his house, to let everybody know that no Jew could be touched. They were afraid of us. As a matter of fact, they were talking about us like we were a whole unit with cannons and everything.

We lived in the forest like animals. We went out every night robbing with guns and we took what we wanted. So we had plenty of food, nobody was missing anything. But the days were like sitting in a prison. Except that in a prison you're not afraid for your life, and here we were afraid every minute, especially in the winter, because the Germans and Ukrainians could follow your footprints in the snow. We had to move to different places a number of times. I stayed there, fighting in the woods, for about eight months until the Russians came and

"THOSE WHO SAY
WE SHOULD
FORGIVE
AND FORGET,
HAVE NOTHING TO FORGIVE
AND NOTHING TO FORGET.
I CANNOT FORGIVE.
I CANNOT FORGET."

liberated us in March 1944.

Several times I was almost caught because I used to go out during the day to see people I knew in the villages and sometimes even spent nights there. My family had had a wholesale store before the war and when we were taken to the ghetto, my father left all kinds of merchandise with some Ukrainians that he knew. I would bribe the camp commander and leave in the middle of the day to bring them food and other things in the ghetto. At night, I would leave the camp again and eat with this peasant couple.

When we were liberated, I joined the Russian army. As a matter of fact, I liberated my wife—whom I hadn't yet met—from Chernstichov on January 16, 1945. I was in a special unit of the Russian army border police devoted to catching the murderers. We were like the German soldiers, except now the roles were reversed, surrounding houses and looking for all those bastards. We worked day and night. They were scared as hell of us. When we came into a little town you could hear people saying, "Close the houses, the Russian Gestapo is coming." I certainly felt like I was getting my revenge. I remember one general kneeling in front of me, begging me, saying, "I didn't do anything."

One thing I will never forget. In one of our stores, we had had these shelves with a wall of drawers in front of them. The whole unit could be moved. My mother fell and broke her leg when the war started and she couldn't walk without a cane. So we put a couch behind the false wall, and when we'd hear that the Germans were coming, we'd put her in there with water and run away to the forest.

Once, when I was with the Russian army, we were looking for an SS man around Katowice. Knowing how the Jews had hidden, I was designated the specialist in finding out where people were hiding. We walked into this store and it was the same setup as my family had had. I said to the Russians, get ready with your machine guns. And I started to take out the wall of drawers, and sure enough the guy was there with food and chocolate and everything.

The Holocaust is always with me. I look at things differently than others. I still have dreams, less than I used to, but I still have dreams. When I went back two years ago, standing in the place where they came to kill us, I showed my daughter and grandson, "This is where my ashes are supposed to have been."

WHEN MY FATHER LEFT VIENNA, the Germans had already occupied the city. The *Anschluss* [annexation of Austria by Germany] was in March, and my father had left a few days before. He was a writer and a journalist. He had difficulty getting a job; in 1938, there was already rampant anti-Semitism in Austria. He had had jobs in Germany, in Berlin, as editor-in-chief of several newspapers and magazines, but he had to quit when Hitler rose to power. We had been living with him in Berlin at the time. So we moved from Berlin back to Vienna, which was just a matter of returning to our homeland. We had no means of economic support, however, so we moved in with my grandparents.

My father tried to support the family with all kinds of activities. He was an editor of what was called the *Salzburger Festspiele*, which was a newspaper covering the Salzburger festival. But his writing was known to be antifascist, and when the political situation in Austria got questionable, he was put on the Nazi blacklist of intellectuals. He knew he would be taken to concentration camp, so he decided to go to Prague. Once there, it became clear that the Germans would soon occupy Czechoslovakia, too. My parents considered all sorts of plans, even going to Madagascar, but in the end my father settled on France.

My Latin teacher in Vienna was very Catholic, but I think she had a Jewish boyfriend; she was antifascist, so she wanted to leave Austria, too. When she learned that we had gone to France, she wrote, asking if she could come stay with us. Of course, we said yes. And so she came and stayed in our apartment in Paris. When she started looking for a job, she saw an advertisement for a German teacher in Le Chambon, a small village in central France. She got the job and moved there.

In 1939 my father was sent to a detention camp as an enemy alien, because he was Austrian. The French didn't distinguish between Jews and non-Jews. Since they were at war with Germany and Austria, Austrian citizens were enemy aliens. My older brother, who was seventeen, was also sent to a detention camp, a different one. My father was finally liberated because some people had vouched for him. He came home in 1940 and then left Paris. And my mother and I were essentially left alone.

We had to decide what to do. I was in art school at the time. We ultimately left Paris, but it wasn't easy. My father lived in a very tiny village called St. Sauveur-Parmelac, and we went to stay with him. Meanwhile, my Latin teacher, Hilda Hereford,

wrote to my father suggesting he send me to Le Chambon because it was known to be a safe place for young people. She could arrange for me to stay with the pastor. He agreed. I arrived in Le Chambon in the summer at the age of sixteen.

Le Chambon is part of a plateau that was settled by the Huguenots about 250 years ago when they fled to escape religious persecution. They were Protestant Christians in a Catholic country. In order to be able to exercise their religion freely, they settled way, way up in an unknown region that was difficult to access. Because of that history, the Huguenots knew the word "refugee." They thought of themselves as refugees, and they understood what it meant to be persecuted for one's religion. And their history, combined with one of their deepest beliefs—that the Jews were the chosen people, G–d's people—made them ready as a group to welcome Jewish refugees.

Pastor Tormé, who was their spiritual leader, had no difficulty translating this into action. When the persecution of the Jews began, he organized other communities—like the Quakers and the Swiss—to help him to rescue Jews, especially Jewish children.

When I arrived in Le Chambon, I worked *au pair* for Pastor Tormé's children; it was my job to keep them happy during their summer vacation. His oldest daughter, Meli, was no longer a child; she was fourteen at the time. The next child was Jean-Pierre, he was twelve. But the other children—ten-year-old Jacob and seven-year-old Danielle—were in my charge.

At the time I arrived, there were no other Jewish children there yet. But Pastor Tormé was in touch with various organizations, such as the Red Cross, and the Quakers, and they organized visits to the concentration camps. They suggested to parents there that their children would be safer in Le Chambon. If the parents agreed, the children were sort of placed under the authority of these neutral organizations. Pastor Tormé had tremendous foresight to do this.

Le Chambon already had a history of helping children. For many years, sick children would go there to recuperate, because the air at that altitude was very good. It was the sort of place you went after you had TB. Later, they started a school for these children, which was why they were looking for a German teacher. So based on this background, Pastor Tormé created one of the first children's homes for refugee children, La Gespi. When he established the home, he asked me to transfer there because many of the children didn't speak French, and I was bilingual.

"THE MOST MEMORABLE THING WAS THE FIRST SANDWICH WE GOT IN THE UNITED STATES . . . WITH WHITE BREAD."

Mostly, the children came from the concentration camp of Gurs in southern France, near the Spanish border. They had been transported there from Germany about a year earlier. Gurs was one of the earliest French concentration camps; it was actually established for Spanish refugees from Franco. Since the Germans wanted Germany *Judenrein*—free of Jews—they just deported Jews to France. So they sent entire families to Gurs. This is where Paster Tormé thought he would be able to save a lot of children, and he was right.

My main task was to listen to these children, to help them overcome their misery, to interpret their misery, and to bridge the two cultures. I don't think many people realized how unhappy the children really were. I mean, from a general point of view they were saved, but they had been wrenched away from their families, and they were very disturbed. The young children cried all night; there were boys who were so hungry they just ran around the house howling. This was wartime France, and food was scarce.

But this part of France was not yet occupied by the Germans. That came later, after I'd already gone. I stayed in La Gespi with the children until November 1941. It was then that I received a letter from my father saying we had gotten a visa to America. We went to Marseilles, where we had to wait for the papers to leave France: it wasn't sufficient to have an American visa. One day my father said, "This is taking too long," and he decided we were going to leave France with or without permission. On December 7 we crossed the Spanish border just before the frontier closed behind us. So the Spanish couldn't send us back. We finally got passage on a boat to America in February. I always thought it was the last passage out of Europe to America, but I later learned later there was one more boat. We landed in Norfolk, Virginia.

Eventually the Nazis heard about Le Chambon and came in search of the children. One of the houses where there were hidden children was denounced by collaborators. At the time Daniel Tormé, the pastor's nephew, was in charge of that particular house. When the Nazis took the children, Daniel—a young man in his twenties—went with them. He was so attached to the children that the Germans believed he was Jewish, too. He went with them to the concentration camp. . . .

Interestingly, Le Chambon was later used by the Nazis for soldiers recuperating from injuries. So the remaining children there had to be kept completely hidden at all times. Not only was the operation totally underground for about two years, but they continued bringing more children in. And they helped not just children. I think the figure that's quoted is five thousand—five thousand Jews that were helped by the people of Le Chambon. At some point, the danger for the children became too great and they were smuggled out, to Switzerland or wherever they could get to.

It wasn't one person, it wasn't two persons, it was the entire spirit of Le Chambon that protected those children. This spirit is unique. I don't know of another instance where a whole population launched so solidly an individual—yet cooperative—effort to combat evil. There was no real coordination, no one person who was responsible for anything. I believe it was due to that solid background of faith. I took that spirit with me from Le Chambon, and am grateful, almost, for the experiences that gave me the opportunity to get to know people like the people of Le Chambon. They restored the dignity of every person they took in. And that was perhaps in the long run their biggest contribution. They gave us back ourselves.

TOM LANTOS	*Birthplace* Budapest, Hungary	Rescued by Raoul Wallenberg
Occupation Democratic congressman from California		*Current residence* Washington, D.C.
ANNETTE (TILLEMANN) LANTOS		*Birthplace* Budapest, Hungary
Protected by the Portuguese embassy; Switzerland		*Current residence* Washington, D.C.

ANNETTE: Both Tom and I were born in Budapest. My husband comes from a family of teachers and professors, and I come from a business family. Our families knew each other before the war. We kept in touch throughout the Holocaust. We were both only children.

Persecution and oppression prevailed in Hungary ever since the end of World War I, really, but deportation did not start until the Germans occupied Hungary in March of 1944.

Tom, at the time, was living with his parents and going to school. Right at the beginning he was inducted into forced labor camp, and taken to areas that had the heaviest Allied bombardment. The young men from the forced labor camps were not allowed to go into the air raid shelters during these raids. Tom wrote me letters during the air raids, saying that everybody around him was dead, that he was the only survivor. He always said that when it's all over, he's going to stand up and walk away, which is exactly what he did.

TOM: My correspondences with Annette gave me a purpose. We knew we would get married, and obviously this gave me a tremendous goal to live for.

ANNETTE: Tom escaped seventeen times from forced labor camp, but they would find him and bring him back. Finally he was successful, and he made his way with a friend back to Budapest. This was in October. Tom's house was razed by the bombs. We don't really know what happened to his father. His mother escaped through the air raid shelters, underground. But very soon after that, she was taken on one of the forced marches to Auschwitz, and we never heard from her again.

Anyway, when Tom came back, he found out that his aunt and uncle, to whom he was very close, were living in a Wallenberg house that was part of the international ghetto that Wallenberg protected. And so Tom went and stayed with them.

TOM: I was sixteen and an active member of the underground, and my story is no different from anybody else's who was in the underground. Because if the Hungarian Nazis or the German military suspected you, they had a very simple formula of ascertaining whether you were a Jew or not. They made you pull down your pants; no one was circumcised, except Jews.

But since I was totally Aryan looking, a tall, blond, blue-eyed boy in a sort of Hungarian paramilitary uniform, I looked very much the part of the master race. That gave me a cover

and some license to do all of the things that literally hundreds of people were depending on. I was moving all over the city at a time when the Nazi bands were chasing and hunting Jews and killing them. I brought food and medicine to the inhabitants of the house who couldn't leave.

ANNETTE: Wallenberg was this Moses from the north. We had no idea who he was or why he was there. He would go out every day, following the forced marches, and when people fell down and the Nazis moved in to shoot them—because if you couldn't keep up, you were shot—Wallenberg would jump in and say, "I'm a Swedish diplomat, and this person is under the protection of the Swedish king. If you shoot him you will be accountable to the Swedish embassy." Every day he would bring back dozens and dozens of people.

Later, when we started working for Wallenberg, we discovered that two days before the Germans evacuated Budapest, the seventy thousand people in the ghetto, and the twenty-five thousand people in the international ghetto—protected by the Swiss, the Swedes, and the Spanish—were surrounded by machine guns. The SS troops were ready to dynamite all of these houses and liquidate the last remaining Jews of Budapest

When Wallenberg discovered this, he went directly to the German headquarters, not to the SS but to General Schmidt-Hueber, the general in charge of the regular defense forces of Budapest. Wallenberg told him that the SS were about to slaughter all the people in the ghetto, and that if the general allowed this last-minute slaughter to take place, he, Wallenberg, would see to it that Schmidt-Hueber would be held responsible after the war. When Schmidt-Hueber heard this, he kicked Wallenberg out of his office, saying, "You have no authority. You don't represent anybody. I can shoot you here and nobody will know the difference." To which Wallenberg replied that before he left his office he had sent a cable to Sweden telling them where he was going, what he was going to say, and who was responsible for his demise in case he didn't return. So Schmidt-Hueber gave the orders to dismantle the dynamite, and he stopped the SS from wiping out the ghettos of Budapest. Of course, the ghetto residents never knew.

My husband was the author of the bill that gave Wallenberg honorary American citizenship. That was his first legislative action when he got into Congress.

My story is different from Tom's. My father was very, very

prominent. He had a jewelry store that was the equivalent of Cartier or Tiffany, and he was very philanthropic, a center of the community. He was in forced labor camps from 1942, and my mother and I were at home alone.

My cousin—Magda Gabor, the sister of Zsa Zsa and Eva—was the secretary to the Portuguese ambassador. And so my grandmother called her and said, you have to take in Marianne and Annette. So we were in hiding in the Portuguese embassy. Later the ambassador gave us Portuguese passports.

Then all the ambassadors were withdrawn. All went except for Wallenberg. And because of Wallenberg, the Swedish embassy stayed in Budapest until the end. The Portuguese chargé took us and my aunt and uncle with him to Portugal. We drove through Austria, and then amazingly enough we were allowed to enter Switzerland. But they kicked us out of Switzerland to France.

Then there was another counterattack by the Germans, and my mother was very concerned, so I had to go back to Switzerland alone. It was Christmas Eve, 1944, and I was thirteen years old. At the border that night, I watched the guard from behind a tree walking up and down. When I saw that he had gone a long distance, I pulled open the barbed wire and got into no-man's-land. As I was walking I suddenly felt the ground give way under me. It turned out there was a river there, which of course I could not see because it was frozen over. And so the next thing I knew I was in the water in my big heavy coat, which had filled with water and was pulling me down. Luckily the water was only as deep as my shoulders.

By that time the French, the German French, heard the noise and came to look for me with floodlights. But by the time the lights focused in on me, I had managed to get through the second barbed wire fence, which took me into Swiss territory. A Swiss soldier was waiting there for me with

a gun. Holding the gun to my chest, saying "Halt!", he took me by the scruff of my neck into this little guard house. When he saw I was a child—I was very small—he was a little less harsh in his treatment. Because of my age, they did not return me to France. I had friends in Switzerland who vouched for me, and I stayed there until December 1945, when I made my way back to Hungary, alone.

I knew Tom was alive, because the war ended in May and by July I had a letter from him. He must have found out from my uncle where I was. So I went back and didn't find anybody except Tom and my uncle. My mother had remarried and was living in Paris. Tom and I sort of cleaved to each other. We were all that was left of our past. And then in 1947 he got a B'nai B'rith scholarship to come to the United States.

TOM: The impact of my experiences during the war made Annette and me totally committed to human rights as the most important goal to work for globally. That is the single issue we have been involved with in Congress more than any other. It's also why I've been cochairing the Congressional Human Rights Caucus, which I cofounded with Congressman Porter. It's why I served as chairman of the Human Rights Subcommittee, and now I'm the ranking member. Because human rights are, in fact, the fundamental issue of human dignity from Tibet to Cuba.

It's not the same as political democracy, of course. Political democracies are a political system, a structure. Political democracies are more likely to observe human rights than other systems, but clearly we were a political democracy while we had slavery. So political democracy doesn't ipso facto mean that everybody has human rights. It merely means that those who are eligible to vote are functioning within a democratic system. And there are historically non-democratic systems that nevertheless have had considerable respect for human rights.

From the point of view of the individual, human rights is clearly the single most important criterion of the quality of his life. It is what enables him to move freely, live freely, speak freely, worship freely, function as a dignified and civilized human being. And there is no doubt in my mind that had I not had the ultimate deprivation of human rights during the war, as a persecuted Jew, I would not have been this profoundly convinced of the importance of this issue.

"I NEVER EXPECTED TO SURVIVE. I JUST LUCKED OUT. EQUALLY COMMITTED PEOPLE WITH EQUALLY GOOD COVER FINISHED IN THE DANUBE. IT WAS A DAILY LOTTERY WITH DEATH. AND I HAPPENED TO WIN."

~ TOM LANTOS

"NOT ONE BULGARIAN JEW DIED FIGHTING THE NAZIS DURING THE WAR. I MEAN, THEY DIED FROM OLD AGE AND FROM ACCIDENTS, BUT NO ONE WAS PURPOSEFULLY SENT TO HIS DEATH BECAUSE HE WAS A JEW."

I WAS BORN IN BULGARIA BY MISTAKE, because my mother and father and two uncles were already living in Palestine, having gone there in 1933. They were Zionists. But my parents decided to visit my ailing grandparents in Bulgaria in 1937, and then the borders were closed and they couldn't return.

My first real memories date back to 1941, when I was three years old. There was no persecution to speak of, and as far as I can remember, it was perfectly safe to go out on the street. I remember my father taking me to a playground in the middle of the city, in the autumn of 1941. And he left me playing in a sandbox in the playground while he went to the bank across the way.

Although Bulgaria was allied with Germany, it did not participate in the war. Rather, what Hitler preferred—at least at first—was for Bulgaria to provide food for the eastern front. Things didn't start to get bad for the Jews until later. Toward the end of 1942, beginning of 1943, restrictions were imposed, and the Nuremberg Laws were adopted. From then on it was dangerous. The faces of people started to change. They started worrying about what was going to happen.

It was a unique situation in Bulgaria. As a child, I didn't sense the danger until we were evacuated from Sofia in May of 1943. I was five years old. In three days we had to pack up and leave. Initially we were supposed to be taken on trains to Poland. But those plans were canceled, and instead we were simply evacuated from the capital.

The Bulgarians were really not anti-Semites at heart—the government was pro-German and so on, but the people were not. In fact, they protested very seriously. In 1943 members of Parliament stood up and said that they didn't agree with people being deported, that these people were Bulgarian citizens.

The Church was supportive, too. On the day of evacuation, the Brataslav Bulgarian Church, which is Eastern Orthodox, said, "We are going to open the churches to every Jew who wants to come. And if they want to take the Jews, they can take all of us." One of the bishops from the town of Ploviv went so far as to say, "If any train comes here, I will lie down on the tracks."

The evacuation was a gesture to comply with the German request for purity, an alternative to deporting us to Auschwitz, the original request. However, many of the Jews from Macedonia and Greece, territories which were administered for the Germans by Bulgaria, did go to Auschwitz. And those trains passed through Bulgaria.

On one of those trains was a Jew from Bulgaria, a pharmacist, who had been sent to serve Bulgaria in a camp in Macedonia or Thrace. And when the deportations of these Jews to Auschwitz started, he was rounded up, too. When the train passed through Bulgaria, he started shouting and he was recognized. There was such a stink made; they took him and all the Jews who had Bulgarian citizenship off the train.

Why did they allow the Greek Jews to pass through? In my opinion there was absolutely no choice. Eichmann's deputy was in Bulgaria. There was a quota of twenty thousand people for that transport. And there were only twelve thousand Jews in Macedonia and Thrace. So they wanted to take eight thousand Bulgarian Jews to fill the quota, which is when the whole thing initially erupted.

We went to my father's village, Provadia. My father was taken to work camp. It wasn't slave labor; they were like the Jewish regiment of the Bulgarian army. They were charged with the construction of roads and railways. They worked ten hours a day, for which they received food points.

But it isn't luck that saved us, it's history. Since Bulgaria attained its independence from Turkey in 1878, the Jews became emancipated as well. They thought of themselves as Bulgarians. They helped the Bulgarians gain their independence. Two hundred Jews were killed serving in the Balkan wars in 1904. They never separated themselves from the rest of the population. They were not very religious. Ninety-nine percent didn't wear a yarmulke. And although they would not eat pork, they were quite liberal in their kosher arrangements. So there was a closeness between Jews and non-Jews.

What I remember most from the evacuation period is cooking and baking and playing cards and gossiping. The kindergarten was the street. We would venture out to the small river that flowed through the town and throw stones and try to fish. There was no war. The war was in Sofia.

My parents were worried, but they had no idea that any killing was going on. They just talked about being resettled in a different country, making plans in case we were sent to Poland. In no way was it felt that there was a chance they might be killed.

When we left Sofia, Bulgaria was forced to declare war against the United States and Britain. As soon as they did, the Allies started bombing. One-quarter or one-third of Sofia was destroyed, but because of the evacuation, there were no Jews there. We'd all left. That was a twist of luck.

After the war, three thousand Nazis and collaborators were executed in Bulgaria. Within a year it was done. And all confiscated property was returned to the Jews.

GERTRUD MAINZER | *Born* March 13, 1914 | *Birthplace* Frankfurt am Main, Germany

Westerbork; Bergen-Belsen | *Occupation* Retired family court judge, practicing attorney, teacher at the Benjamin N. Cardoza School of Law | *Current residence* New York, New York

I GREW UP IN quite an intellectual family. My father was one of the founders of German labor law and a criminal lawyer and very politically active in the Social Democrat movement. That's why when Hitler came into power in 1933, we had to leave Germany. They immediately arrested my father and placed him in prison. He was released after about ten days, and we left shortly thereafter. Because my father had taught law at the University of Frankfurt, he was able to get a similar position in Leiden and Amsterdam in Holland. Ultimately, though, even Holland was not far enough.

My husband, who was one of my father's students, had followed us to Amsterdam, and we got married in 1936. We had two children—Gabriele and Frank. And then on May 10, 1940, Hitler invaded Holland.

The Germans arrested my husband practically immediately and accused him of helping Jews to take money out of Germany without the permission of the German government, which, of course, was true. That's how we were separated. He was taken back to Germany, placed in prison in Hamburg, and I stayed behind in Holland with two small children.

He was actually lucky that he was picked up for legal, not political reasons, which became the rule very soon thereafter. Since he had a very good attorney in Hamburg, which had remained a comparatively democratic kind of city, he was able to get out of prison after a year and a half with the stipulation that he emigrate from Germany. I had in the meantime obtained Cuban visas for all of us. My husband wanted to come back to Holland and have us all leave from there, but I didn't want him to take the risk. I just wanted him to go and for us to follow if possible. But we couldn't get out.

In 1942 one of my father's students, Floris, a non-Jew, took it upon himself to find hiding places for all of us—my grandmother, my parents, one sister, myself, and my children. We all went into hiding in different places. This student found a place for the children with two Christian women who had actually always had a home for children. When the Germans came, the two women decided to take only Jewish children, because this way, they could save their lives. So they took in about ten Jewish children. And Gabriele and Frank Mainzer became Marijke and Frank van den Burgh.

I hid with a family in Dordrecht, not far from Rotterdam, called Traarbach. He was a bookkeeper with a very small income, a socialist, very outspoken. For him, taking me in was a political

act against the Germans. She was a housewife without much education but with a heart of gold. Previously, they had no Jewish friends or connection with Jewish issues. One day, Mrs. Traarbach saw Germans arresting some Jews on the street. Suddenly she realized this could have been her child. So without even telling her husband, she talked to her physician, who she knew worked in the underground, and told him that she wanted to help. I arrived, as Toni Bowers, in August 1942.

The whole Traarbach family arranged their lives around me. They stopped seeing friends. They stopped sitting in the front room, which had windows to the street. They stopped having any help at all to clean the house. We built a hiding place in a closet so that in case of danger I could disappear completely. We divided a clothes closet into two parts with a wooden separation. I jumped into the back part of the closet whenever the doorbell rang. We also listened to the radio in there. At night, when it was really dark, the Traarbachs' daughter would take me out for a walk. I learned all about the moon. On moonlit nights, we couldn't take our walk.

I had no idea where the children were hiding, just in case the Germans found me and would try to force me to tell them where the children were. None of us knew where the other family members were hiding. Floris, who visited each of us once a month carrying letters from one to the other, was the only one who knew.

In the summer of 1943, Floris brought the children to the Traarbachs for one night. Gabi was six years old and Frank was four and a half. Gabi recognized me immediately, and said, "Look, here is my tooth." She had lost a tooth, and she had kept it for me. But when I said to my son, "Frank, do you want to wash your face with mommy's face cloth?" he said, "Is mommy here?" I said, "Don't you know me?" He said, "I have never seen you in my life." My heart broke, but I didn't tell him I was his mother. What was the point? All he talked about was how he wanted to go back to his "aunts." Gabi realized that Frank didn't recognize me; she never said, "Mommy" during that visit. She was already Frank's protector.

One night in the middle of the week in September 1943, Mrs. Traarbach made a whole plate of little fried fish. "What's the occasion?" I asked, and that's when they told me that Floris had gone to the home in which the children had been hiding and found it empty. The Germans had taken the two women and all the children first to the prison in Amsterdam, and then to Westerbork.

Later on, when I asked Gabi what had happened, she didn't

"AFTER TWO YEARS OF SEPARATION MY SON HAD NO IDEA WHO I WAS.

want to talk about it immediately. Two or three months later, in Bergen-Belsen, she said, "Mommy, sit on my bed, I will tell you." She told me how the Germans had come and how they tried to find out from the children where their parents were. She had always said, "I don't know." Then the Germans would say, "What did your parents talk about when they were alone?" hoping to get a clue. Gabi said, "When my parents wanted to talk, they would send me out of the room," which, of course, had never been the case, but even at six, she felt the danger. But for Gabi, the worst part was when Frank had to go into the hospital barrack at Westerbork, where she could not visit him because she was too young. "That was the worst, because I had no one to take care of anymore," she said, a mother already.

I decided to go join the children. Everybody tried to talk me out of it. They said, "You don't jump in the lake when you cannot swim, when you know the people are drowning and you will drown with them." But Mrs. Traarbach didn't try to discourage me. She understood; she was a true mother.

I was told that if the Germans were to find out I had been in hiding, I would be sent immediately to Auschwitz. But friends of mine discovered that if you could prove you had relatives in the United States or other parts of America, you might be sent to a new camp, Bergen-Belsen, instead of Auschwitz. People in Bergen-Belsen might be used as exchanges for German POWs. But you had to have proof of American relatives. Since no Red Cross letters from the Western Hemisphere could get through anymore, my Floris stole Red Cross stationery and forged a let-

ter from my husband to me. With this letter I went to Westerbork, but even today, I don't remember anything about how I got into Westerbork except that it was on February 24, 1944, a day the commandant was off duty, and one day after my son's fifth birthday. I had hoped to be there on that day, but I was told the commandant had to be out on the day I was smuggled in.

The letter worked, and we were transported to Bergen-Belsen in April 1944. Bergen-Belsen was located in the middle of Germany, in the Lüneburger Heide. Instead of green pastures, there was a dried-out piece of land with long rows of barracks. It wasn't that crowded at first. We each even had our own little wooden plank on which to sleep. The children, of course, stayed with the women. We had such illusions that we even started to set up a school for the children. In the beginning, we tried to be very civilized.

The daily roll call could last anywhere from two or three hours to all day, depending on whether a child had fallen asleep in his bed or someone was too sick to get up. We stood for hours in rows of five until the Germans counted the number of people they knew they had in the camp.

Bread became the most valuable possession in the camp. When Frank had no more shoes, I gave a woman six portions of bread for a pair of children's shoes one of her children had outgrown. And I myself got a few portions of bread for a woolen dress. I still feel guilty to have taken bread from a starving person. Even today, I still feel bread is holy.

We spent the last two months of the war in a Red Cross camp in the south of Germany. It was surrounded by chicken

BUT A MOTHER IS A MOTHER.

AND THERE IS NO QUESTION HOW FAR A MOTHER GOES."

wire, but on the other side there were fields and farmers who plowed their land with horses and a wagon. I took my children to the edge of the chicken wire and said, "See, there is freedom." I thought they would know what that means. The first day after we were liberated by the French, we walked out of the gate. Suddenly Frank yelled, "Mommy, here walks freedom," pointing to a horse. He thought the word for horse was freedom.

Not only did I learn that the concept of freedom is not inborn, but also that the transition from slavery to freedom is very difficult. On our first day out of the camp, I couldn't get Frank to step off the sidewalk to cross the street—that step was completely unknown to him. Even I had great trouble taking this step, accepting freedom. My brother, who had fled to America from Belgium, was in the U.S. Army, stationed in Frankfurt am Main, and he had found our names on a Red Cross list of concentration camp survivors. When he came to take us with him out of the camp on June 21, 1945, I was so scared of meeting my husband after all that had happened, of having a normal life, that I didn't want to leave. He said, "Okay, I'll come back tomorrow." He slept in his jeep. When he came back the next day, I was more reasonable.

Since that time, the idea of freedom has become most important to me. Everybody thinks freedom is something inborn, but it isn't. It is something that has to be taught and experienced, and that is why, for me, the experience of the Holocaust showed me what it means to be free. Here, everybody takes freedom for granted, as though it were no issue at all.

There is no question that my children were affected by the Holocaust. When we were reunited with my husband in Cuba, my son said, "Mommy, after we leave, where do we go from here?" The idea that you could stay in one place was completely removed from his mind. Another time he asked me, "Mommy, can you make it again so cozy as in Bergen-Belsen with the candles, the white tablecloths, and every Sunday a piece of wurst?" I only realized later what he was referring to. I had some sheets that without water I couldn't wash, so I tore them into pieces to use at the latrine and to put under our dry piece of bread so we wouldn't have to eat on a dirty blanket. There was no electricity, so I lit some leftover candles. As for the wurst, once we got a rotten piece of liverwurst, and that became for him "every Sunday a piece of wurst." For him, all of his experiences became a fairy tale.

My daughter, on the other hand, still today refuses to talk about it. When her children ask me about the Holocaust now, she still says, "Mommy, not in front of me." She had to carry it all, become numb and never show a reaction while she was the caretaker of her brother during the time they were alone. It was the only way she could survive. And that has followed her all her life. The only time she allowed herself to show her feelings was the day of our liberation. While everyone was outside, happy and laughing, I found Gabi on top of the barrack bed crying like a baby and saying, "I want to go to my Daddy. I want to see my Daddy." During all the previous years she had never been able to talk about her father. Freedom at last had loosened her numbed heart.

B E N J A M I N   M E E D | *Birthplace* Warsaw ghetto | Survivor of the Warsaw ghetto and an
active member in the Warsaw underground | *Occupation* Retired exporter; president of the American
Gathering of Holocaust Survivors; president of the Warsaw Ghetto Resistance Organization; chairman of
the United States Holocaust Memorial Museum Content Committee; chairman of the annual Yom Hashoa
Commemoration in New York for the last thirty-two years. | *Current residence* New York, New York

THE WARSAW GHETTO uprising: On April 19, 1943, Passover, about five hundred Jewish men and women, with few weapons and no military training, fought off more than two thousand well-armed German troops for more than two weeks.

I WAS BORN IN POLAND, in Warsaw, into a middle-class Orthodox family; not from the very rich, not very poor. We could trace back our Warsaw roots 253 years. We were a family of around three hundred people. My great grandfather had eighteen children, my grandfather had nine, I am from a family of four; maybe six out of all of us survived. I had one brother and two sisters. One little sister survived. Our family was wiped out, my roots were wiped out.

I am a graduate of the Warsaw Business School. I was less than twenty when the war began. I was in the underground in Warsaw as a Christian boy, together with my wife Vladka. She is the so-called Heroine of the Holocaust. She doesn't like to be called that, but she was the major courier of the underground. I was involved in building all the bunkers in which people hid. A lot of people are, thank G–d, still alive because of these bunkers.

I participated in both the Jewish and Polish uprisings. Thank G–d the Poles didn't know I was Jewish. If they would have, I don't know that I would be sitting here today. There was an uprising in 1943 and another in 1944. I was in both. In 1943, the Jewish people were liquidated. Before the war, there were 350,000 Jews in Warsaw, but most perished. There were a thousand synagogues, yeshivas, medical schools, engineering schools, you name it, it was a tremendous life. We had the most organized Jewish life. There were a thousand house committees. Everything was illegal, but we had yeshivas, we learned, we had cultural events, we tried to keep our dignity all the time. We buried documents for safekeeping, so they could be dug out after the war. None of us thought we would survive, so we had documents, for history.

My wife and I could have gone into hiding. We were exposed to danger every minute of every day in our work. Every hour, every minute, I thought I wouldn't make it. Today, if I think back on what we were doing, I cannot explain why I did it, endangering myself more. It was an instinct.

When I walked on the street, everybody who looked human was my enemy. I couldn't trust the human race at all anymore. I could have passed by a righteous person, a righteous gentile maybe hiding Jews in his house, but for me, he was a human being, so he was my enemy. The only things of which I was not afraid were dogs, cats, and horses.

The day of the 1943 uprising, I was on the Aryan side. We were supposed to stone the ghetto, but we never did. The whole center of the city was burning, and nobody gave a damn. Normal life was going on, and across the street people were burning alive. I will never forget this. A carousel was playing. Children were riding on it, almost in the vicinity of the burning ghetto, music was playing. People were burning alive, and nobody even dared to say stop the music. You could see the flames a hundred miles from Warsaw.

When I was liberated, I thought I was the only person in the world. Wherever I went, everything had disappeared, a whole life disappeared. Warsaw, Poland, is for us one great cemetery. Burned ashes. I could not remain in this cemetery.

Vladka and I came to this country in one of the first boats in 1946, very young, without a family, without luggage, with $8 in our pockets. And we rebuilt our life. We have two children. Both were born in the United States. They are both physicians, and they married two physicians. I have five grandchildren. To some extent, my children are my *nekama*, my revenge; my grandchildren are definitely my *nekama*. I chose life instead of hatred.

"SURVIVORS CAN SIT DOWN AND TALK ABOUT CARROTS OR FLOWERS AND SOMEHOW, THE CONVERSATION ENDS WITH THE HOLOCAUST."

ROBERT MELSON | *Born* December 27, 1937 | *Birthplace* Warsaw, Poland

Posed as Polish nobility | *Occupation* Professor of Holocaust History, Purdue University

Current residence West Lafayette, Indiana

MY MOTHER'S MAIDEN NAME WAS Natalia Ponczek. She was born in Warsaw, Poland, in 1914. My grandparents sent her to the Warsaw Conservatory of Music, where she studied voice and piano. When the depression hit Poland and money was scarce, she got a job as a singer at the Adria, a well-known Warsaw cabaret.

My father, Wolf Mendelsohn, was born in 1906 in Austrian Galicia. He had lost his mother to tuberculosis during World War I and was left alone in a Swiss boarding school when he was ten years old.

Even before the war, he was posing as a non-Jew. In Poland, Jews were not allowed to carry on business with the state. My father's business required that he deal with the Polish government, so he started calling himself William Melson. People thought he was Swedish. In fact, when my parents first met, neither one thought that the other was Jewish. When I was born, I was sort of a Polish poster child—blond curls, blue eyes, pug nose.

On October 12, 1941, all the Jews were supposed to assemble in the center of town. We were to bring one suitcase per person, and we were going to be resettled. On the appointed day thousands of Jews, families with kids, aged grandparents, with their bags, their pets showed up. They were piled into trucks and taken outside of town to the Jewish cemetery. There, they were lined up and machine-gunned to death, their bodies tumbling into predug ditches. This was the work of Einsatzgruppe D, one of the special killing squads appointed to implement the final solution.

My parents had our bags packed. But that morning, my mother woke up before dawn from a dream. She had seen her father holding a sign with the number 12 on it. He had whispered, "Danger, danger," and then turned to face a brick wall, which gave way to a bright white light. She woke in a panic and insisted that we shouldn't go, but rather that we should go into hiding. I was four years old.

My parents remembered a couple they'd met at the Unionka café during the Russian occupation—Count and Countess Zamojski. The place had been crowded and the two couples were seated together. It so happened that they had a son my age, little Count Boguslaw. Although they had a famous name, they were penniless. The plan was that my mother would go to the Zamojskis and offer them whatever we had in exchange for their birth certificates and other papers of identification. With these documents, we would leave the city, posing as them.

They agreed, but they wanted more money than we had. Somehow, my mother managed to get a look at the papers—the countess left her alone with them while she went to bring in the tea. My mother took her key and etched as many details as she could onto her leather handbag.

The next morning, she went to the local church and asked to speak to the priest, hoping that he wouldn't know or remember the Zamojskis. She explained that during the Russian occupation all her family's papers of identification had been confiscated and that now in particular it was crucial to have them. The priest quizzed her on all the particulars, and then excused himself and returned with the precious birth certificates. One for her, one for my father, and one for me. Her gamble had paid off.

For the next four years in Kraków, Prague, and Vienna, we were the Count, Countess, and little Boguslaw (Bobby) Zamojski. My parents once had a close encounter with an old man who had known the real count and countess, but luckily, his eyesight was failing. It wasn't until after the war, in Brussels in 1945, when I was eight years old, that my parents told me my true name and that I was Jewish. The Zamojskis never found out that we had been impersonating them.

"MY MOTHER WAS A REAL CHARMER, SEXY AND BOLD. AND SHE KNEW HOW TO PLAY A ROLE. DURING THE WAR SHE IMPERSONATED A POLISH COUNTESS, SOMETHING HER LOOKS AND HER BACKGROUND HELPED HER TO DO."

ERNST W. MICHEL | *Birthplace* Mannheim, Germany | Several labor camps; last stop—Auschwitz, from which he escaped at age 22 in April 1945 | *Occupation* Journalist; former executive vice president of the United Jewish Appeal in New York | *Current residence* New York, New York

MY JOURNALISTIC COLLEAGUES were all young Germans carefully chosen by the Military Government. I was the only Jew among them. They regarded me with something close to awe when they learned of my background. I was Jewish, though I didn't parade that before them, because I didn't want it to get in the way of our working together.

I couldn't have concealed it long, because in addition to my regular assignments, I was asked to write some personal stories under the byline "Special correspondent and Auschwitz survivor, #104995, Ernst Michel." Less than six months ago I was an inmate in a Nazi concentration camp, and now I sat in the courtroom at the Nuremberg Hall of Justice.

I had a regular assigned seat in the press section. To my right were eight judges, two each from the United States, the Soviet Union, France, and England. On the left were two rows with the twenty-two defendants, including Hermann Göring.

I was the only Holocaust survivor to serve as a reporter at the trials, and many American and British newsmen wanted my reaction. Sometimes I wanted to jump from the press gallery to shake the defendants by their shoulders and yell in their faces. "Why did you do this to us? Why did you kill my friend Walter? Why did you hang Leo, Janek, and Nathan? Why? Why?" It wasn't easy to keep my personal feelings separated from my job as a reporter, but fortunately, in addition to my regular assignments, I was given the opportunity to write a few feature stories, where I could vent some of my emotion.

As part of my assignment, I was to interview some of the defense lawyers. I had several interviews with Dr. Stahmer, Göring's chief defense counsel. One afternoon, at the end of the proceedings, he took me to the sparse prison cell where Hermann Göring passed his time. There was a bed, a small table that held a photo of his wife, and a chair. That was all. It was a far cry from the opulent palace where the high-living Reichsmarschall threw his famous parties.

The meeting was arranged with the condition that it remain off the record. I was nervous. What should I say? Should I shake hands? Ask questions? Since I couldn't write about it, why did I want to go through such a painful experience?

Göring stood up when Dr. Stahmer and I entered his cell, which was constantly under guard. "This is the young reporter you asked me about," Dr. Stahmer said, motioning to me.

Göring looked at me, started to reach out to shake hands, and, sensing my reaction, turned away for a moment. I stood frozen.

What the hell am I doing here? How can I possibly be in the same room with this monster and carry on a conversation? How could I talk logically, unemotionally?

Mr. Göring, how does it feel to be here? What do you think of the proceedings? Are they treating you well? Should I shout at him, tell him that he was responsible for my six years in the camps? Should I blame him for my lost childhood? For the death of my parents?

I did nothing of the sort. I stood there and stared while Dr. Stahmer discussed the next day's proceedings.

Then, on an impulse, I bolted for the door and asked the MP to let me out. I couldn't take it. I couldn't remain. I had to get away. There was no discussion, not a word was exchanged, no comments or statements were made. I was there, and then I was gone. Period.

NUREMBERG, February 20 (GNS)–I have a book in front of me. A picture book. But not a picture book for children. A book which in Russian carries the title "International Military Tribunal, Nuremberg" and on the middle of the bindings says "Auschwitz Camp." The last two words are underlined.

The book has no preface at all and very little text. As I said it is a picture book, but a picture book of reality. And it is simply "exhibit no. such and such." Nothing more. And the Russian prosecutor who introduced it in court doesn't say much about it.

In fact, that isn't necessary at all, for these pictures speak for themselves. They speak of the life–or rather the death–of the prisoners at the Auschwitz concentration camp, which was the largest of all German concentration camps.

Three miles from Auschwitz there was Birkenau. A nice name, giving the impression of a birch wood, an opening in it and a small, quiet village. But that was not the Birkenau that I am speaking of. The Birkenau near Auschwitz was something different. It was a camp where about 100,000 prisoners were quartered–one can't say "were living."

And behind this Birkenau camp there were five large smokestacks, which were smoking steadily. These were the five giant crematoria and the four giant gas chambers of Birkenau, which were working day and night, where not tens of thousands, not hundreds of thousands, but millions of human beings were gassed to death. That was our Birkenau.

And my glance rests again on the little picture book with the title "Auschwitz Camp."

There is the electrified double-barbed wire fence with the sign "danger" and the death's head, the wire into which 20 of my co-prisoners were driven in one night.

I am leafing through the book and see another picture showing a large blackboard. This blackboard used to hang in the staff headquarters at Auschwitz and listed the daily changes in the numbers of prisoners. The board in the picture is dated Jan. 16, 1945, the last day it was used. The number of prisoners that day was 10,224. And the next day 9,000 of us began to march along the icy roads of Upper Silesia, "fleeing" from the advancing columns of the Red Army. The remainder was left behind–they couldn't march any longer.

And when we arrived at Buchenwald after three days of marching and five days of travel in open freight cars in blizzard weather, there were but less than 4,000 of us left.

The book is finished. It is again in front of me. I pick it up. It doesn't weigh much. But it is the history of millions of my co-prisoners, and today, here at the Nuremberg trial, where the bill is to be paid, it weighs much, very much.

~ STARS AND STRIPES

In the Warsaw ghetto, in the beginning, we used to go on what we called "runs." The Germans would open the gate to let in a garbage truck or something, and fifteen or eighteen of us boys would run. By the time the Germans took up their rifles, most of us were over on the other side.

Life in the ghetto was survival of the fittest. Nobody had the time or the means or sufficient crumbs of bread to share with anybody else, even the little ones. We ran to get something to bring back to our families. We didn't think about the danger. We had a dictator in our stomachs—hunger. We used to have a joke, "If they nail me, you can have my shoes."

I knew enough people. So many a time I would deliver papers. But I never thought of myself as being part of the underground. I was a flat carrier. They needed me, I was there.

When the fighting started in the ghetto, the power against us was a million to one. The German philosophy was simple: Is someone positioned in that building? Burn the whole darn thing down. But it became a matter of dignity. By running we were fighting. By being chased we were fighting. And so in spite of the disparity of power, it took over forty days for the ghetto to fall.

When I was on the Polish side, some of the Poles looked at the Jews and said, "The Jews are fighting! Isn't that something? The Jews are fighting! The Jews are not being soap any more." A few people survived; mostly by going through the sewers. But even then, the Poles were waiting on the other side, ready to give you away.

During the final fighting in the ghetto, I was captured and taken to Ponwator, a labor camp. My family had all been taken to Treblinka by then. Miraculously, I escaped from the camp. I managed to get back to Warsaw and got in touch with a friend who was a shoemaker.

Through the shoemaker, I met a couple of people who went into business manufacturing cigarettes. So I bought cigarettes from them and started selling. I sold to the Germans, the Poles whoever, officers. We were about twenty boys. We met at Three Crosses Square. Everyone had their own corner. There were always Polish boys who tried to give us a hard time. So we roughed them up a bit and chased them away. They used to call me Bull because I pulled them all together.

The Germans used to buy a lot of cigarettes on the black market. They were rationed in Germany, too, and they never got enough. Of course, they wanted foreign cigarettes, so we would wrap some of them in fancy paper. We would make sure to sell those imitation cigarettes as a train was leaving, so by the time a soldier realized it, he was gone.

Everybody was hustling and trying to get the most out of a deal. We each found different places and markets. We were close, but we were competitive. You had a customer, someone else was trying to take him away. I tried to tell them the money's not everything, that one of these days we will all be shot anyway. As we made a little bit of money, it became a little bit better. But once you make some money, you become more cocky, take more risks. We started selling newspapers in the city itself.

We could have been killed, but we thought we walked on water. We would buy a quart of liquor and sit down, youngsters, from ten to whatever, and drink. We used to say we drank to kill the worm in us. Maybe it helped.

The youngest of us, Bolus, was eight or nine. He stuck to me like glue; I guess he looked at me as a brother or uncle or something. He used to sing on streetcars, such sad songs about orphans and war. Some of the other kids would steal his money or take his stuff. One day, the police picked him up off the street; not as a Jew, but because he had gotten into a fight. We became afraid. The other boys and I looked like Poles, but he looked more Jewish, and we couldn't shake him. Finally, I had him taken off the street.

A widow by the name of Zofia Kalot let us stay in the alcove of the attic in which she lived. We were eight, ten kids sometimes. It was just like a box. One person moved, everybody had to move. We used to quietly sing ourselves to sleep with Polish songs.

"THE POLES HAD AN EXPRESSION. THEY'D SAY, 'FROM NOW ON SOAP IS GOING TO GET EXPENSIVE, BECAUSE THERE ARE NO JEWS FROM WHICH TO MAKE IT ANYMORE.'"

IF YOU SAW ME in the street you wouldn't say I'm a Jew, you would say I'm an Italian. I was named Gastone in honor of my father's brother. He was killed in World War I. He got an honor medal, called the Gastone; my family was very proud of my uncle, who died serving his country. That's why I say I was an Italian boy, a Livorno boy like all Livorno boys. We had maybe three hundred Jewish families in Livorno, with characteristics like the characteristics of all Italian people. There was no differentiation. The only difference was that once a year my father used to write a letter to the principal of the school to excuse my brother and me from religion classes. And I used to go to synagogue with my parents and grandparents, for Yom Kippur, for Pesach, for other occasions. We used to go to the Jewish school to learn history or to play with other Jewish children, but these were not my friends; I saw them only on these occasions. And I think that my situation was absolutely typical.

Things started to change in 1937, which is when the first anti-Semitic articles appeared in the Italian papers. In August 1938 I was in Rome because I was representing my city in the national youth games as a runner. By the end of 1938 a number of laws were instituted. When I came back to Livorno, I was not able to attend public school anymore. My aunt who taught at the public school was dismissed. My grandfather had the most important pharmacy in town, and he had to sell it. My father couldn't find work. It was a real shock. We felt completely isolated. All my old friends and my parents' friends disappeared because they were afraid. To be seen with Jews or to help Jews was dangerous, so they had to protect themselves. This is normal. I don't condemn them.

We had difficulties, but no physical danger. Italy was better for Jews than a lot of other countries. Only nine thousand Jews were deported, out of about forty thousand—less than 25 percent. In Poland, it was more like 98 percent. I was called with the others, some twenty boys, to forced labor nearby. My father had gone to France to find work. Then, in 1942, when Germany occupied all of France, my father was arrested and sent back to Livorno, to jail, where he stayed until May 1943, when he was sent to a camp in Italy. Not a death camp, but a concentration camp. Livorno was bombed, and we moved to the countryside.

My father was freed on July 25 with the fall of Mussolini, and he joined us where we were. When the Germans took over in September, we had to flee. We were on our way to Florence, where someone was supposed to help us reach Switzerland, when the Germans took over. So we stayed for a month in a convent, sort of like a pensione for old priests in Florence. Then we went to the mountains near Norcia, between Umbria and Marche. We found a hiding place, and we spent the worst moments of the war there. I taught in the village nearby—Italian, Latin, and mathematics. And my brother, my cousin, and I joined the resistance.

The Pope never denounced the persecutions. But many convents were open, and they did provide sanctuary. At a certain point, the priest in charge of the convent I was in came to me and my brother and cousin, and told us that the Germans were looking for Jews in Florence in all the convents and churches and it was dangerous for us to remain, but if we wanted to stay, they had prepared a safe hiding place for us. It was our decision to go to Norcia.

In 1938, when the ration laws were implemented, we had a problem with ourselves and our identity. I mean, at that moment I realized that I was different. I realized that I was a Jewish boy and what that meant. I was not particularly observant; I had felt that I was like other people, and I wasn't. Why? I thought, should I remain like I was? Should I baptize and become Catholic like the others around me?

A group of twenty or twenty-five of us, young Jews, boys and girls, used to meet in secret to discuss what to do. Should we remain Jews and be persecuted? Would our children be persecuted again? And then the children of our children? Or should we forget about being Jewish? At that moment we knew that this wasn't anything new; Jews had been persecuted all the time in Italy. We started studying about Judaism. Finally, all of us decided to remain Jews because we thought that being Jewish was a kind of culture as well as a religion. But we also worried about whether we should go to Palestine or remain in the diaspora. Maybe there was a reason for us to spread ourselves around the world.

Our identity as Jews was established at that moment. It has never been the same since. I don't know if I would have married a Jewish girl if not for that moment—probably not, because my life was so integrated into Italian life.

I WAS AMONG THOSE whom the Holocaust sought to consume and somehow did not.

The *somehow* is my story. It involves the strange mechanisms of chance, one person's almost unaccountable bravery, and an eventual decision to dedicate myself to something that has been, all the while, inseparable from that self.

When the dark, empty future of the Jews was plotted by Hitler, I was a very small child in Poland, and as that plot was brought into action, I quickly became—I would later learn—one of the "hidden." I was one of those children who found themselves in the care of righteous non-Jews, who built bravely upon their religious principles and manifested their love of others by taking the condemned into their homes and hearts—when most other non-Jews were passively standing by, some actively collaborating.

Hiding, I was to learn years later, had meant life.

I recall a street. I recall the house in which I lived—in which I was loved by the Catholic nursemaid with whom my parents had left me in the hope that I would thus be saved from the horror they knew was to come. That woman taught me much—especially, ultimately, a lesson about moral courage and what it can accomplish. The acts of such rescuers took place during a time when courage could be viciously punished if discovered—and chance of discovery was always impending, often from the information of a nearby source.

Growing up, how many times I asked myself "Why me?" Why did I survive when so many others—children as well as adults—perished in the gas chambers, by fire, or by the bullet? Why was I one of those fortunate enough to be protected by bravery and love in a world filled with cruelty and death?

I knew that we, who were in the midst of it all and had survived, must somehow serve as witness—to the horror that had stepped into our lives and to the bravery that had preserved and freed us. I knew that the deepest ideals and most immediate concerns of the Jewish people must be ever-present at the core of my life. It was left to those who survived to represent and defend the traditions, hopes, and visions that the Nazis had tried to eradicate forever.

As a young man in America I came to work at the Anti-Defamation League (ADL) fresh out of law school. I eagerly hoped that through my work I could accomplish these visions of mine, specifically in ADL's law department, whose work is so largely a dedication, a mission that underscores daily the vitality of our people. My years on the league's legal staff—and later in its leadership—have seen the sometime flourishing of old evils, such as in the renewed publication of the *Protocols of the Elders of Zion* or in the charge that Jews were behind the Communist movement, as well as the emergence of new and vicious thrusts, such as the accusation that Jews dominated the African slave trade. The league has also exposed and countered one of the foulest doctrines that ever could be preached: the claim that the Holocaust never took place at all.

Surveys of anti-Semitism in the United States have produced of late a certain paradox. In my years at ADL, such surveys have shown a slight but steady decline in anti-Jewish attitudes, possibly in part an effect of the passing of older persons with older perspectives, together with a proportional growth in the number of younger, more enlightened, less prejudiced persons. But while anti-Semitic prejudice has declined by about one-third during the last three decades, ADL's annual compilation of anti-Semitic *incidents* has shown a steady increase in recent years—particularly, and disturbingly, on college campuses. Personal threats, harassments, and assaults against Jews rose nearly 250 percent during the last decade. And so the paradox: against a decline in anti-Semitic attitudes expressed generally, there has appeared a tendency among hard-core anti-Semites to act in direct confrontations.

The brighter side comes for me, ironically, out of the darkest memory. One of my most gratifying days ever at ADL—surely one of the more memorable of my life—was a Sunday in May 1991, when out of history's awful shadows came an amazing blaze of light. I was pleased to have been the keynote speaker before 1,600 people at the First International Gathering of Children Hidden during World War II—the birth of our Hidden Child Foundation/ADL. This was a climactic moment for the young boy who had remembered that home in Poland, the Catholic nursemaid, and the incredible moral courage and compassion that had enabled thousands of children to survive. Here in New York were 1,600 of those children, who represented and remembered the traditions, dreams, and courage that must be preserved in memory.

Everything to which we are committed at the Anti-Defamation League has its roots, I believe, in the determination that children must never have to be hidden, ever again.

Abe Foxman is currently the Executive Director of the ADL.

ANNA ORNSTEIN | *Born* January 27, 1927 | *Birthplace* Szenbrô, Hungary | Auschwitz survivor | *Occupation* Psychoanalyst and faculty member of the University of Cincinnati Medical School | *Current residence* Cincinnati, Ohio

THIS WAS OUR SECOND stay in the death camp. The first time, only two or three months earlier, we were in a different part of the camp, in a more primitive unit. Now, on this second stay, we were in an older, more established unit of Auschwitz. The barracks were huge; there were probably more than a thousand women in each. Every afternoon we got our bread, which had to last through the next day, and every morning, a warm, thin soup. We also got some marmalade with the bread once or twice a week, and on Sundays there was stew made out of horse meat. It was under these much improved circumstances that we were told about being tattooed.

Early in the morning—I believe during *Appel*—we were told that we would be tattooed that day. This immediately raised our hopes: it was definite proof that the Germans intended to keep us alive. The tattoo meant that we would be sent out of Auschwitz, work somewhere, be away from the crematoria....

I remember the weather as generally dry and pleasant that fall of 1944. The day we received the tattoo was, I know, a particularly brilliant day. It was some time midmorning, when we were taken to another part of the camp. We could see from the distance three or four tables standing in the middle of the road, with two uniformed girls sitting at each of the tables. They looked very pretty to me; they had hair, they were not skinny and dirty like us. Their navy blue uniforms gave them status and importance. As we learned later, the girls were not German but Jewish girls, fellow inmates from Czechoslovakia. They were a privileged class, well fed and well clothed.

We formed long single lines in front of each girl. Discipline must have been at the minimum. How else could I have roamed about to see which of the girls did the neatest job of tattooing? But I did just that and I found "my" girl. She was short, had dark hair and a friendly smile. I wanted my numbers to be small, well-shaped, and on the inside of my arm. I was seventeen, and that day I prepared myself for life. Most of the girls put the tattoos on sloppily: big numbers at a distance from each other, not in a straight line, carelessly on the outside of the forearm. When I got to "my" girl, I told her that I had observed that she of all the girls did the best job of tattooing. This obviously pleased her, and she rewarded me with the smallest, neatest tattoo in the bunch. I recall trying to keep up a conversation with her. I very much wanted to be confirmed in my optimism, to be told that the tattoo really meant that we were to live.

The tattoos gave us some sort of an identity. In camp, we had no names. We were not "registered" anywhere with our names, birthplaces, and ages. The number on our arms was our only distinction, and we gave it added significance by thinking that it would save us from extermination.

On the whole, I am no longer conscious of my tattoo, but feel apologetic when I realize that it evokes unpleasant feelings in my friends. The tattoo reminds them of something they would rather forget. Whenever I perceive their glances at my arm, which to me indicate their discomfort, I would like to explain my tattoo to them. I would like to tell them that the day we received the tattoos was a good day for us; that we had received them as if they were passports to life.

People often ask me about my children's reactions to the tattoo. I don't believe they noticed it for a long time. To them, it was like a mole, like a birthmark. Or maybe they thought that all mothers are numbered? By the time they knew this was not something I was born with, they knew the story. But I do recall a question my son Rafael asked when he was about six years old: "Mother, are you sure you didn't do anything wrong when they did this to you?" For a six-year-old, the world has to be just; goodness should be rewarded, and only bad people should be punished.

MY MOTHER AND I were sent to Rivesaltes, the camp in southern France that would become the hellhole for Jews in Vichy France. In Rivesaltes, things got really bad.

Even though around us people were getting sick and dying, we kids would still play games. One child I played with a lot was a boy by the name of Savic.

Around Passover 1941, my mother and Savic's mother began talking to us in hushed tones; they wanted the two of us to escape. I guess they must have been getting reports about what was going on in Germany and Eastern Europe and what was going to befall the Jews. I don't recall ever questioning why my mother wouldn't come with me. She told me she would escape later and meet me at a certain place, and I accepted that.

At the last minute, Savic's mother backed out and didn't want him to go. And this was when I really saw my mother's courage. She decided that I was going to escape even if Savic wasn't. The date she chose was May 1, which in Europe was Labor Day, a holiday, so she assumed that there would be fewer guards around. She told me which area in the camp to leave through, how far I would have to go before hitting a highway, and to follow that highway to Perpignan, a city fifteen to twenty kilometers from Rivesaltes. There, I was to take the train to Marseilles. And in Marseilles, I was to go to a Jewish social services agency. She had a little bit of money, I don't know from where, and she gave it to me.

Come May 1, I put on twice the amount of clothing I normally wore and took along a potato-sack-type bag to pretend that I was going to gather pieces of wood. My mother and I said our good-byes in the barracks. She didn't accompany me because she didn't want to draw attention to me.

I crawled under a fence and kept crawling. I knew there was a train trestle that was somewhat elevated, and that if I could get beyond that, I would be out of the vision of the camp and the guards. In fact, my mother had been right; there were fewer guards than usual, so it wasn't difficult for me to crawl out between two guards' positions.

Once I got to the train track, I crossed it and ran like hell through a vineyard. I got to the highway and walked along the ditches until I got to Perpignan. I went to the train station and bought a ticket, but the train wasn't scheduled to leave for a number of hours, so I decided that the best thing for me to do was to hide in the public toilet.

When I got to Marseilles, I went to the Jewish social services agency, and within a day or so, I was sent to a home for refugee kids in southern France—in Boulouris. There were about thirty of us kids there in a big French villa. I was there for almost a year.

I got letters from someone who had written for my mother—she must have gotten in touch with the people in Marseilles, who told her where I was—and indeed, she had escaped from Rivesaltes, too. But she felt I was safer where I was. Then the letters stopped.

The following spring, I was informed by one of the social workers at the children's home that my mother had been captured and taken back to Rivesaltes, but that she had put my name on a list of children to be sent to the United States. So they prepared me to go back to Marseilles.

When I got to the gathering place in Marseilles, lo and behold, there was Savic! It was a real reunion. Before they shipped us out, the French authorities allowed the people from Rivesaltes whose children were being sent to America—namely my mother and Savic's parents—to come and say good-bye to us. It was spring 1942.

My last meeting with my mother was very tough. It was clear that my chances of seeing her again were poor, but I was a pretty optimistic kid. I didn't think that it was the last time I was going to see my mother. Perhaps I was denying the truth. But it was the adults who knew that drastic things were about to happen; we kids were not really informed. And I guess, probably, we also didn't want to find out.

Savic and I decided that we would stay together. They asked us where we wanted to go. We didn't know. We didn't know America at all. All we said was that we just wanted to be together. So they shipped us to Pittsburgh, where there was this Jewish family—the Wagners—with three daughters, who agreed to take us both. I don't know how they did it, because Mr. Wagner drove a bread truck. Savic and I were together for a year, and then they found another family for him.

I had no news from anyone. I know now that I was really isolating myself from what had happened in Europe. Because even though the war had ended, I made no effort to find out if anyone—my mother, my father, my brother—was still alive. I found out from Savic, who had been receiving letters from his mother, who was in southern France, that my mother had died. But I didn't pursue that information.

I was drafted and sent to Germany in the early 1950s. I also went to the village where Savic's mother and younger brother lived. Savic's mother told me that my mother had been among the many people from Rivesaltes who were sent to Drancy and from there to Auschwitz.

"OF COURSE, THE WAR COMPLETELY WRECKED JUDAISM FOR ME. I WAS REARED IN AN ORTHODOX FAMILY. DURING MY TEEN YEARS, I BECAME COMPLETELY ATHEISTIC. NOT ONLY ATHEISTIC, BUT OTHER THAN SINGING IN SYNAGOGUES TO HELP PUT MYSELF THROUGH SCHOOL, I STOPPED GOING [TO SHUL] EVEN ON HIGH HOLIDAYS."

~ HENRI PARENS

JACK POLAK	*Born* December 31, 1912	*Birthplace* Amsterdam, Holland	Westerbork;
Bergen-Belsen	*Occupation* Chairman Emeritus of the Anne Frank Center U.S.A.; knighted by Queen
Beatrix of the Netherlands in 1992; investment banker	*Current residence* Eastchester, New York
INA POLAK	*Born* January 3, 1923	*Birthplace* Amsterdam, Holland	Westerbork;
Bergen-Belsen	*Current residence* Eastchester, New York

JACK: One Saturday afternoon in 1943, I went to a friend's birthday party. As I came in I saw this beautiful young girl sitting there. She was much younger.

INA: Ten years younger.

JACK: So I saw this beautiful girl. I talked to her, and that was it. This was in June 1943. I was taken away in July 1943, along with most Dutch Jews. We were picked up in a civilized way, by Dutch police, not Germans. I was sent to Westerbork, a Dutch deportation camp. Once there, I found my father and mother, who had been taken earlier. After two weeks my father and mother were taken away. I gave my father my new shoes, because his were old. "You have to work," I said, not knowing that two days later he was going to be killed. My parents died in the gas chambers of Sobibor. I became principal of the school in Westerbork from July 1943 until February 1944.

I met Ina again in September 1943, when the last Jews of Amsterdam were rounded up. Her father had been president of the Jewish community in Amsterdam, a community of about a hundred thousand. Everybody knew him. Ina and I started courting each other, walking along the Boulevard of Misery. When we couldn't see each other, we started writing letters.

Three kinds of trains left from Westerbork: cattle cars to Auschwitz, trains to Theresienstadt, and trains to Bergen-Belsen. To go to Bergen-Belsen one had to have certain privileges. Ina's father was in diamonds. And the Germans wanted to create a diamond industry, but they needed the Jewish skill; they needed those Jewish diamond workers to be preserved. So many were sent to Bergen-Belsen.

Another group was made up of people to be exchanged for German POWs in Palestine. For that purpose they made a list of people who had been active in the Zionist movement. I was on that list. I went to Bergen-Belsen in February 1944; so did Ina.

But here, there was almost no way to see each other. So we exchanged love notes, which were written on little pieces of paper. But they were letters of hope and strength, and they gave us both something to live for.

INA: He sometimes brought the letters at night. Or I used to go and make his bunk, because he had to get up at three. He would leave a note for me. And I would leave a note for him.

But I was taken from Bergen-Belsen on April 7. After six days and nights on the train, we ended up at the Elbe River, practically on the front. You could hear the shooting. Later on we learned that the order had come from Berlin to drive the train into the river. But there were two thousand Hungarian Jews on the train. They had come late to Bergen-Belsen, and still had gold hidden in their clothes. So they bribed the train commander. Before afternoon, we were liberated by the American troops.

JACK: I was taken away in a cattle car on April 9, two days after Ina. I knew that Ina had gone, but I had no idea where. I didn't know what happened to her. I didn't know if she was alive. We traveled all through Germany for two weeks. Because I had been working in the kitchen I was still pretty strong. I had not deteriorated like the rest. So I had to carry out the people who died on that train for fourteen days. On April 23 at six o'clock in the morning, we saw strange uniforms. They were Russian. And we were free. I was liberated in Troebitz, near Leipzig. I didn't know where Ina was, and she didn't know where I was. All I knew was that I wanted to get back to Holland.

INA: The Americans who liberated us sent us back to Holland in May of 1945. We traveled in these open freight cars for two days in absolutely beautiful spring weather. We arrived tanned.

JACK: I returned to Holland in July.

INA: He had lost all his hair from typhus. He didn't have too much hair to begin with, so he was quite a sight. I thought, "My G–d, is that what I'm going to start out with?"

JACK: In September we got engaged.

INA: October.

JACK: In October we got engaged. In January 1946 we were married.

"IT WAS A WAY OF LIFE WHERE YOU WERE TREMBLING EVERY MINUTE."

June 7, 1944, Wednesday evening, 8:30

My dearest Ineke,

Just a few words from my bed. Remember darling, be smart and don't get sick. We just can't have that here. If it happened, I would have to violate all strict rules and set foot in Barrack 17!! But hopefully, that will not be necessary. Everybody is all excited about the invasion, and, of course, I am, too. Mostly because at moments such as these our future becomes tangible. I, of course, had my dreams before, but everything seemed so far away, because nothing was happening. Now it is as if our chances are closer at hand, and at the same time along with that come all the optimistic thoughts that I had for a happy future for both of us. Do you feel that too, darling? Maybe it is extra good that we feel this way, because it will get harder for us here by the day, with each success of the English. I had a small example here today at the shoe factory where you could feel the Germans' lousy moods, but it is especially then that my ties with you make it so much easier to carry on. I am dead tired; thus, only these few thoughts for you.

Sleep sweetly, be all healthy tomorrow, much, much love and kisses,

your Jaap

March 5, 1945, Monday morning

My dearest boy,

When you depart, quietly say good-bye. . . . Yes, my boy, now it is actually coming. Precisely when, we don't know yet. People say that we first must be deloused and that the machine for it still has to be repaired. Furthermore, there is a diptheria case in our group, and a scarlet fever case, which is quite a scary thing. But I don't think it will hold us up. People say that we are going to Liebenau, and some say via that camp to Switzerland, but nobody knows exactly. We only hope for the best, and are counting a little bit on it. Thank G–d Lita is improving, and Dr. A. said that with future good care, she could be better in three months. At the moment, it is a strange situation here. We are eating every bit of the small supplies that we still have, but if it takes too long, we will have nothing left to eat. . . . Dearest boy, now I am really going to take my leave, thus I will end this letter, because I don't know how to say good-bye. We know it all, and that is enough! Keep your head up high, and I have strong hopes that we will be together very soon.

Much, much love, good kisses, etc.,

your Ina

"THE LIBERATION WAS LIKE A FALL THAT HURTS, BUT SOMETHING INCREDIBLE HAPPENS TO YOU AND YOU FORGET THE PAIN AT THAT MOMENT. AND THEN IT COMES BACK, WORSE THAN EVER."

ON THE NIGHT OF THE BOMBARDMENT of Rotterdam, we sneaked out and crossed the border from Holland to Belgium. We came to Antwerp and found a place to hide through some cousins who did a lot of business in Belgium. The idea was that we would stay there until they could find us brokers to take us by train out of Belgium into free France—southern France was not yet occupied.

We found the brokers and decided we would go in small groups. My husband and I were the first to go. The next day my parents and my sister would go, and the following day, my brother. My husband Sol and I embarked on our trip, hoping for the best, but very soon thereafter the Gestapo stormed the train and took almost everybody out, including my husband. I sat there in a panic; I guess I had turned ashen. The brokers were sitting with me in one place and my husband was sitting in another. They thought it would be safer that way.

I saw the Germans take Sol away, and I was frozen in space. They didn't do anything about me because I looked so Aryan. No sooner did the train start to move than, of course, I started to scream that I wanted to follow him. And the brokers held me back, saying, "Why? Then you will be dead, too. You have to go on. We will bring you to freedom." And I said that we had to turn around and warn the family in Antwerp immediately of the horror that awaited them, which we did.

I think one of the most horrifying moments of my life was my return to Antwerp. Because when I went back to warn my family, my brother, Yo, was there, and when he saw me coming, he started to scream. My father and mother had just left with my sister. And when he saw me, he realized what was happening.

My brother and I decided to stay in Belgium and hide. At one point, my brother was living over a barbershop and I was living with this wonderful family with two young girls. I wanted my brother to meet them. Well, he came over and the mother of the house loved him right away. So we both ended up staying there.

But my brother began to compete with one of the boyfriends of the oldest girl, Colette. He was careless. He took her out on the town and tried to live a somewhat normal life. Of course, the boyfriend went immediately to the Gestapo and denounced us.

One day when I returned from a walk, the Gestapo had been there. My brother had jumped over the wall of the garden and was on the run. But I had to disappear now, too, because they knew there was a sister, and they had somehow found out that I had long red hair.

I ended up living in this house in the suburbs with some cousins—a doctor and his wife and their baby—along with some other Jews. But I didn't feel safe. So one day, I asked my brother to come over and bring me some money so I could leave. I wish I'd never asked him. . . . We were waiting for my brother, and out of the blue I got up and said, "I'm not going to wait. I'm going to get out of here now. We are not safe here. We all ought to go away from here." They laughed and told me not to be hysterical.

But I felt so strongly that it was unsafe that I pleaded with my cousin to give me the baby. I felt we had been there too long. We were too many Jews in one place. And there were too many neighbors. But they wouldn't listen. I didn't even go upstairs to get clothes or a toothbrush.

I called Colette to let her know I had left, and she started screaming that they were all taken, including my brother. He was picked up on the street on his way to bring us the money.

My brother was put on a train to a concentration camp outside of Antwerp, called Mechelen. They were warned that anyone who tried to jump off the train would be shot right there and then. Well, my brother was a tough one; he jumped. He lay in a ditch for a day or so, and when he was sure it was safer, he managed to get to a farm. He told them his story, and they helped him and took care of him until he could walk properly. When he returned to Brussels, Colette told him where I was.

Colette's mother found us a small little stable way out in the country in Masbourg. It was like an ointment for the many, many wounds we had, and although we were desperate for our family, at least we had some kind of life for a little while.

One day a young fellow from the village rode up on his bike and said, "The Germans are in the village. We don't know what you are, but we wanted you to know." And so we went into the woods. It was raining so hard my brother turned blue. He was trembling, and trembling, still weak from his time under Gestapo arrest. I lay down on top of him in that soaking rain. I was afraid he would die. We were lying there for hours, until somebody came and told us they had gone. It turned out to be a false alarm. They had only come to buy cigarettes. But after that, we carried a kitchen table deep into the woods to lie under the next time we had to flee.

ON MAY 15, 1940, there was an illegal transport from Bratislava in Yugoslavia to Palestine. I paid 10,000 *krons* to the Batir, the Jewish organization to get onto this rebuilt tugboat. We were packed like sardines. The boat was an old wreck, and when we got to the Yugoslavian border, they wouldn't let us continue. Finally they let us pass, and we exchanged one old tugboat for another old tugboat at the Romanian border.

There were 512 people on that boat, plus crew, and living conditions were horrible. We could only come up for air at night, and it could only be a few people at a time so as not to upset the balance of the ship. We were on that boat for four and a half months. We went to Salina on the Black Sea, passed the Dardanelles, near Turkey, went on to Greece in the Mediterranean, and from there in the direction of the British blockade and the shores of Palestine.

We were forty miles from Asia when the engines exploded and the ship was disabled and capsized. There was a wind blowing, so we used sheets as sails. After midnight, we put down anchor near a cliff of what we later found out was the uninhabited island of Camilanesi.

Everyone got off the boat. In the morning, we went back to the ship to get people's belongings and food. Luckily we found a cave with drinkable water. We wrote SOS on sheets with shoe polish, and spelled it out with rocks on the sand. We weren't aware of the danger. Being away from the Germans was the main thing.

After about eight days of this, we saw Italian military planes overhead. Later that night, Italian military officers came and took the women and children on a Red Cross ship to an Italian camp on the island of Rhodes. They came the next day in a military ship for the men. The Jewish community of Rhodes came to bring us bread. The Italians were very humane to us in Rhodes. We were there for eighteen months before being transferred to a concentration camp in Calabria in southern Italy and from there to another camp in 1943.

When the Americans invaded Salerno, I escaped from the camp and remained in hiding in the woods until I was liberated by advancing American forces.

"IT WAS ROSH HASHANA. WE ACTUALLY HAD A SEFER TORAH WITH US WHEN OUR SHIP CAPSIZED AND SOMEONE LED THE SERVICES ON THIS UNINHABITED ISLAND."

BEFORE THE WAR MY FAMILY LIVED in Vienna in a comfortable fourteen-room apartment, part of which housed my father's dental practice. We were fairly well-to-do. But by 1938, after the *Anschluss*, Jews were no longer permitted to work. After my father was forced to close his office in August, he became increasingly depressed.

It was clear we had to leave Europe. In preparation for our departure, my parents had applied for passports and visas, and on the morning of September 30, 1938, they went to pick up their documents. They were supposed to meet again at a relative's home later that day, but my father never showed up. He was found dead at the bottom of the stairwell of a four-story building. It was assumed he committed suicide.

Not long after this traumatic event, we heard that a ship, the *St. Louis*, bound for Cuba, was scheduled to leave Hamburg, Germany, on May 13, 1939. Thinking that Cuba might be a safe haven while we awaited entry to the United States, we shipped a vanload of belongings to a warehouse in New York, packed a few suitcases, and took the train to Hamburg.

My brother, who was eleven at the time, found the scene on the ship very disturbing. Always a sensitive child, he found it odd that people on board were behaving as though nothing had happened. Many of the passengers had already lost family and were leaving behind most of their relatives, who, they must have known, they were unlikely to ever see again. The passengers were unsure of where they would end up or what life would be like, yet many of them acted quite carefree.

The captain of the ship, Gustav Schroeder, although German, was a kind man. Although there were Nazis on board who didn't want the Jews to be treated well, Schroeder insisted that as long as he had jurisdiction over the luxury liner, the voyage was going to be like any other cruise. There would be music and dancing and the best food they could get. He wanted the 937 people on board, almost all Jews, to have a pleasurable trip despite the terrible political situation.

Even before the *St. Louis* arrived in Cuba on May 27, Captain Schroeder became aware that there would be trouble when the liner arrived in Havana. When the ship docked, the passengers were awakened at four o'clock in the morning and told to get ready to disembark. Hours went by and nothing happened. Gradually, the news that something was amiss filtered through to us.

All but a few people on board had purchased visas, at two hundred and fifty dollars apiece, issued by a corrupt Cuban government official who pocketed much of the money. Shortly before the arrival of the *St. Louis*, President Bru of Cuba had decided to put a stop to this practice and announced that he would no longer honor these invalid visas. Thus, only the twenty-nine persons with legal visas were permitted off the ship.

Because most of the passengers had quota numbers for immigration into the United States, many of which were scheduled to come due in the following six months, the American Joint Distribution Committee made numerous attempts to appeal to President Roosevelt and to President Bru to allow the refugees to remain in America. Telegrams flew back and forth, but to no avail. Shortly before midnight on June 6 the *St. Louis* was forced to set sail for Europe—what was predictably a death sentence for three-quarters of the people on board. The Nazis used the turning away of the ship as propaganda to show the world that no one else wanted the Jews either.

On the return voyage, the atmosphere on board changed dramatically. People were crying and depressed, and there were several suicide attempts. Captain Schroeder said he would not return the ship to Germany even if it meant setting it on fire. At the last moment, owing to the efforts of the Joint Distribution Committee, England, France, Holland, and Belgium each agreed to give refuge to a quarter of the passengers. After more than five weeks at sea, we ended up in France. Two and a half difficult years later, with the help of my father's sister, Lena Klinghoffer, and her children (her son, Leon, was shot by terrorists in 1985 aboard the cruise liner *Achille Lauro*), we made our way through Spain and Portugal to one of the last ships to leave Europe for America before the U.S. entered war. We arrived in New York on November 10, 1941, four days before my seventh birthday and less than a month before Pearl Harbor plunged the United States into World War II.

"I DON'T REMEMBER THE TRAIN RIDE FROM VIENNA TO HAMBURG, BUT I DO RECALL THE SENSE OF FEAR AS MY MOTHER, MY BROTHER, AND I WENT THROUGH INNUMERABLE PASSPORT CONTROL POINTS."

I WAS THE FIFTH CHILD of six children of a Hasidic family. I survived with one older sister. When the threat of war began, since my town was very close to the German border, my parents decided to send the younger children to the interior of the country. So they found a cousin of my father's whom I had never met who lived in a town called Szekochinn. They thought in a few days the war would be over. I didn't see that the end of the world was coming. I was nine years old.

I arrived on a Wednesday, and on Friday morning we heard the news that the Germans had invaded Poland. People started running back and forth, closing windows and shutters. And I, of course, was overwhelmed. Saturday morning, very early, we were awakened by fire; the whole village was burning. The Polish army was retreating, and they burned everything not to leave anything for the Germans. My father's cousin wrapped himself in his *talis*, his prayer shawl, and started running.

As we were running, I got separated from my relatives. It was complete chaos. I remember Polish soldiers stripping themselves of their uniforms and changing into civilian clothing, and planes flying so close I could see the pilots inside their cockpits. I took out a very strong stocking from my little suitcase and tied the suitcase over my back, and just kept running and running.

I managed to get to my relatives who lived fifty kilometers away, near Rottenburg, and they took me in and comforted me. After I had been there for maybe a week, they helped me make my way back to my parents. That's all I wanted to do. I came back home between Rosh Hashana and Yom Kippur. I walked in, and my father embraced me and started to cry.

Until 1940 we still lived in our apartment. But then we were thrown out, and that's when the horrors began. They started hanging people in the marketplace. We moved into another house in the worst part of the city. There was no running water, no heat, just two rooms by the river. And there was so much death. Every day people were taken out and hung. And the fear of being taken away was terrible. Because of our very strong belief in redemption, a lot of the rabbis would try to comfort us, saying that these were Messianic times and that any day, any minute, the redemption would come. Things were so bad you had to believe in something.

We heard that they were starting to take the children. They had a list of people who had young children. We had this aunt, Ita, who was married to my father's uncle. And they had no children, so they were not on the list. I used to go and hide at their house at night.

Then we found another place, a windowless closet. We were five, six people, children mostly, boys and girls. Because it was always dark we had candles. We also had some bread, water, and a pot. I must have been in and out of this hiding place for about two weeks. One day I refused to go back.

There was a continuation of horrors, of slowly seeing my parents die of hunger, of worries, and of fear. My mother was a beautiful woman, and one day in 1941 she took sick. She had sores on her breast. I had never seen my mother undressed before. My mother was the provider of food for the family. She was the one who would run to what was left of the marketplace to trade a silver cup, a candlestick, for a loaf of bread. Death was almost a welcome guest.

My father would be very hungry for days and pretend he wasn't, that he had eaten. And the little bread he had, he would take out of his pocket and say, "Look what I have for you children." In the winter, my father made a fire by cutting up the last pieces of furniture that we still had. And he would line up the clothing at night to warm by the fire so that when we got up in the morning the clothing would be warm. That was my father.

The final solution for us came on August 12, 1942. The *Judenrat*, the Jewish council, told us to go into this huge sports arena to be counted. We were told nothing would happen, that we would be counted and sent home. Some people believed, and some did not. Some people did not go. One of those people was my brother, who by then had six children. But to represent the family his wife went. She was afraid that if she didn't, they would start looking for her children.

We were sitting on the grass inside this arena for hours. And then the selection started. We stayed overnight, and it started pouring like the heavens had opened up. The ground became mud. And we were sitting there in that mud. The next morning the selection started again.

I came home on Thursday afternoon. Then my sister Hannah came back. But our parents didn't. They had started to shoot anybody trying to escape from the sports arena; there were dead bodies all over. We didn't know, were our parents selected? Were they shot? I went to my grandfather's grave that night and prayed.

I snuck back from the cemetery, and a little while later my

"GOD CREATED THE WORLD. HE DID NOT GIVE US A CHOICE TO BE BORN. HE PUNISHED ADAM AND EVE FROM DAY ONE BECAUSE HE GAVE THEM A CHOICE. TO EAT FROM THIS TREE OR FROM THAT TREE. WHY WOULD HE GIVE THEM A CHOICE? THERE SHOULD HAVE BEEN BUT ONE TREE OF LIFE."

father came home. My mother followed a few hours later. I'll never forget when my mother came in and my father saw her; it was the first time I ever saw my parents embrace.

The one person who didn't come back was my brother's wife. The last glimpse we had of her was on a truck, pulling her hair, screaming about her children. That truck was taking her to Auschwitz. When I was taken away, I remember people saying I was crazy. Because I was not even fourteen and I kept yelling, "What's going to happen to my children?" Because I had assumed the responsibility for my brother's children.

I was taken in November 1942. They came for my sister, and they took me. My sister was hiding some place. My mother threw herself down at this soldier's boots and wrapped her arms around his foot and begged him to take her instead.

They took me to a school building in a town close by, which they used as a camp for those in transit. My brother lived in that town, and he came to the window of the school with a pot of soup that they allowed to be brought in. And in the soup there was a letter in which my brother wrote not to worry, that I wouldn't be sent away, that they were doing everything they could to get me out of this camp and back to my parents. He said I should be hopeful and pray and that everybody was praying for me. I kept that letter for a long time.

There was a selection in the courtyard. And I was almost selected to be part of a group that was supposed to be sent back. And at the last minute, as if an angel had come, I was pulled from that group and put into the circle to be sent away. If not for that

moment I would not be alive today.

We were sent to Germany. My first camp was Blechamer, a labor camp, where there were mostly French, Belgian, and Dutch Jews. At one point I tried to hang myself. But a friend I made in camp took me off the rope and saved me. She said, "Can you imagine your parents surviving the war and then finding out what you did?"

After about two weeks, we were lined up one morning and put on trains, and taken to this magnificent, magnificent part of the world, the Sudetenland. There were mountains touched with snow. And blue sky. It was a place where people lived. And children ran. Where you even envied the dogs, who could run free.

We were placed in Schatzlar, a camp that had textile factories. We were given coffee in the morning and bread, and we were given bread to take with us to the factory. The whole village worked in that factory to supply the war effort with textiles, uniforms, and so forth. We worked six days a week. On Sunday we would clean the barracks. That's how it was until 1945.

But you know, many times when I look back at that life there are moments that I would like to have today. There was such comradeship in that camp; I was never alone. Because we were the youngest ones, the others protected us to some degree. When they heard something might happen, they would warn us, for example, "Don't get undressed tonight. Sleep in your clothes. They're supposed to take young children today," preparing us in case we had to run. And in the few hours we had off, the older women would teach us arithmetic.

A few days before we were liberated, we knew something was going on because suddenly the SS women started being nice to us. They knew the Russians were coming and that the Russians would be very tough on them. So they said, "Please don't tell them what we did. Protect us." The director of the camp killed his wife, killed his two children, put his house on top of the hill on fire, and then killed himself. He did not want to face the Russians.

After the liberation, when people started to run from one camp to the other, when we discovered that there were other Jews in those camps, I found my sister. Somebody told me Hannah was in a camp only a few kilometers from mine, and we had never known. We made our way back to Poland. Two days after the war was over, I went to a hairdresser and got a permanent.

"I HAVE A BOOK ABOUT THE

LODZ

GHETTO.

SOMETIMES I TAKE IT

DOWN TO ASSURE

MYSELF

THAT ALL OF THIS

HAPPENED."

~PHYLLIS SCHNUR

MY FATHER WAS FROM the Ukraine. He came to Poland in 1918 after the revolution. He met my mother, they got married in 1920, and I was born in 1921. He was an accountant. I always felt like we were from the privileged class, not that we were rich, but we were comfortable. My parents were observant, my mother lit candles on Shabbat, and my father was a socialist–a Bundist–but still, every day he put on *tefillin*. And then my father died in 1936, and my good, soft life changed. Not that I went hungry, but I started to work. I was fifteen.

On the first of September 1939, the war started and right away the tanks came in. We thought it would soon be over, because Poland had a good army. In February 1940 they forced us into the ghetto.

We packed up. We took everything, I don't even remember how, but the best things–bedding, linen, tablecloths–we took. Later on, in the ghetto, when we had no more income, we were able to sell these things. What we couldn't take, like the furniture, we left. We closed the apartment and left the key with the super, as though we would soon come back.

In the ghetto we lived on Kornstrasse, in one room; me and my brother, my mother, and my aunt and her husband and their two boys. One room, no toilet. When it was too cold to go to the outhouse, we had to use a pail. There was no privacy. It was terrible, terrible.

I worked making uniforms for the German soldiers. My mother worked, too. You had to work. If you didn't, you didn't get your soup. I was always the caretaker, because sometimes my mother was sick, and my brother, so I was the strong one. I had to wait in the lines in the cold for food. It was very difficult. Sometimes when I went to bed I wished I wouldn't wake up. When I was a little girl, I was always overprotected. Sometimes I think, how did I do this?

My brother was two years younger than I, and he was hungry, but he never talked about it. He used to read books and never complained. He was tall and lanky, and his legs had swollen up from no food. They wanted to fire him from his job, because he was so weak he couldn't work.

I went to talk to the manager, a Jewish fellow. It was summertime. He was dressed in a beautiful white suit. And I said, "If my brother doesn't go to work, he won't even get the little bit of soup. Please, keep him." And he said, "I don't know." I was crying. And then a German supervisor came over and asked me what was wrong. So I told him. He looked at me and said, "Don't worry. I will give you a card. As long as your brother can come, even if he doesn't work he will get soup." Sometimes in the worst thing you can find something good. I never forgot this.

Finally, it got to the point that my brother was so sick he couldn't go to work anymore. I have a cousin who worked with [Mordecai Chaim] Rumkowski, the head of the Lodz ghetto, and he arranged for a carriage to take my brother to the hospital. I gave him, I remember, bread and a jar of sugar to have when he got to the hospital, and I kissed him and he went. I didn't know that I would never see him again.

One morning, when my mother and I were going to work, we heard people saying they were taking people out from the hospitals. I couldn't understand. I thought maybe somebody had TB and they were afraid of contagion. So we went to the hospital and watched from afar. It was raining. And the Germans were taking people out and putting them in big trucks. Some people tried to jump off. We never saw my brother again. It was 1942.

We cried for a few days, but life goes on. So day after day we went to work and got our soup. And they always took people away–sick people, children. Mothers gave away their children. You can't imagine how you feel when you are hungry, when you are scared. We didn't have children in the ghetto.

We worked and worked. And then again they made a selection. My mother and I got a card to go. But I had good friends from school whose father had some kind of a connection. And they let us stay.

They started talking about liquidating the ghetto in July or August 1944. In the beginning nobody believed them. We thought maybe we would live through it, maybe it would soon be over. We were completely sealed off. There were no newspapers, no radios, nothing, just lines for food that was gone by the time you got there.

Then [Hans] Biebow, who was the head of the German liquidation forces, said, "We don't have work for you here anymore, and the Russians are coming. Why do you have to die from a Russian gun? Come with us to Germany, and you will work for us there like you work here." They were closing everything. There was no more food, no bakeries, nothing.

We had to decide what to do. We prepared to leave. I sewed beautiful bedding and other things. And we started to

happen, I just wanted to be with her. I was screaming when they dragged me away. And how many times now I think about my mother, about how she didn't want to leave Lodz. And then they took her. But I had to make the decisions. Nobody was left. My aunt and uncle had gone to Ravensbrück. We had nothing to eat. Maybe my mother felt something, but what could I do? I did whatever I thought was right. But unfortunately it wasn't right.

After about a week, they took us to the showers. They took away my new shoes that cost me so many bread rations and a little medallion my father gave me. And they cut off all my hair with a machine. We slept outside in Birkenau. As for the people who had already been gassed, they told us they had gone to the Ukraine, to work on a farm and take care of children. And we believed. They were master liars. Some people knew better, but they told no one. I was crying the whole time. Sometimes I think that during those years, G–d just took a little snooze.

We waited. There was the smell of burning feathers from the crematorium. I had heard what it was, but I couldn't understand that they take people to this place and gas them and burn them. It just didn't penetrate. I just lay there crying. Then one day they said that five hundred girls from Lodz, all around my age, were being sent to Ravensbrück.

When we got to Ravensbrück there was a pool, and we had to stand around it naked. There was music playing. The soldiers looked at us to make sure we were normal, that we had no diseases. Nobody was even ashamed anymore. They had taken everything away. We were like animals. Then they sent us to Germany, to Milhausen, a tiny town in Thuringen. There was a factory there, where we made parts for airplanes. Our hair started to grow back. There was no hot water, so they gave us tea to wash our hair.

From there, we went to Bergen-Belsen, another hell. We worked for as long as we could but then we started getting sick. People had dysentery, I was very sick with typhoid. My one desire was to die in a hospital, not like a piece of nothing.

On the fifteenth of April, they announced in every language that the war had ended, that we were free. And I was lying there, coughing and thinking, "The war is over for them, but not for me. For me, it doesn't matter. Because I won't live."

I still believe in people. I'm crazy. After all that happened... But even people who are bad sometimes surprise you.

pack. Then my mother said she didn't want to go. Meanwhile, they were looking for people every day. They wanted to clean out the ghetto quickly. So people went into hiding. One day when they came looking, my mother and I hid in the big row of toilets. We went in the farthest ones from the front door. I was standing in one toilet and my mother in the other. And the Germans came in. We thought they would drag us out, but we were too far in for them to come after us. They were disgusted.

Then we had nothing to eat anymore. We had no family left; I was alone with my mother. We went to the place from which they were clearing out the ghetto. They gave us bread, some for me and some for my mother. We were on one of the last transports. They took us in a trolley to one of those boxcars, you know, like for animals. About my perfect bedding, they said, "Why do you have to take this? You don't need this. It has your name. It will follow with another transport." And of course I believed them. . . .

When they opened the doors of the car we were in, an orchestra was playing. There were musicians in white uniforms and flowers. But far away we saw people with long dresses, some with stripes. They were screaming at us to get out. Then we came to the sign ARBEIT MACHT FREI—work makes you free.

They selected my mother. I didn't know what was going to

I CONSIDER MYSELF VERY LUCKY to survive and also lucky to be a member of a group that joined together to resist the Nazis.

When I was growing up, Vilna was a Polish city. In 1939, under the Ribbentrop-Molotov nonaggression pact, the city of Vilna became a part of Lithuania and was renamed Vilnius. We were under the impression that Lithuania was more democratic and less anti-Semitic than Poland, but we were wrong. In 1940 Lithuania became a Soviet republic. Lithuania and the Lithuanian Communist party were actively involved in Soviet rule. In 1941, after the German invasion, the Lithuanians felt that Germany was going to win the war and they would be punished for collaborating with the Soviets, so they wanted to clean their hands.

The easiest way to do that was to take it out on the Jews.

On the other hand, there was a group of Lithuanians, including the Communist party, who left with the Soviets and formed a government in exile. The Soviet partisans that we were in touch with were Lithuanian. On one hand the Lithuanians were our murderers, and on the other they were our saviors.

When the ghetto was set up in 1941, you could take with you only whatever you could carry. My father was the chief doctor in the ghetto Jewish hospital. He was absorbed in daily work, but he never planned how to save his own family. Whatever happened to other Jews would happen to us. This was the thinking of the majority of intellectuals.

We in the ghetto had to work for the Germans outside of it. I was seventeen, and my big interest was art. Before the German invasion, I went to preparatory school for the Academy of Fine Arts. Now I worked as a sign painter.

During one action, a woman by the name Sonia Rechtig was taken by the Nazis. A Jewish policeman informed the SS officer in charge that she was a concert pianist. The SS officer asked her what she played, and she sat down and played the piano, and they let her live. The Jewish head of the Vilnius ghetto, Jacob Gens, suggested it would be a good idea to save the other artists, using Sonia's case as a precedent. The Germans agreed, so he created a theater and gave us the same type of document as for a skilled worker. I started to do stage designs in addition to my regular work. I loved it.

I painted and did graphic work. I got a second prize in a painting contest. In those days, these things were keeping us alive. One of the most horrible things beside being killed was having your dignity taken away from you, so cultural activities were very important. I also knew I had a limited amount of time before I would be killed.

People told us about a place called Ponary outside Vilnius where Nazi *Einsatzgruppen* and their Lithuanian henchmen were killing the Jews. If there was an action and they took thousands of people, and you were left alive, you gave a sigh of relief: "I made it." And the fact was, that may have been only for a few months.

The Jewish population in Vilnius, including refugees, had been seventy thousand. Now it was twenty thousand, so fifty thousand had already been killed. Nobody from the Vilnius ghetto was taken to concentration camps yet; that only started happening later.

At the same time there was a group of resistance fighters who were preparing a revolt. Everyone knows about the uprising in the Warsaw ghetto, but the idea for that revolt came from Vilnius. A young poet and painter, Abba Kovner, one of the leaders of the Vilnius resistance, read a proclamation on January 1, 1942, calling for an armed resistance. By coincidence, January 1, 1942, was the day I turned eighteen. Abba Kovner was already twenty-three. He had this idea that the goal of resistance should be not only to save ourselves or damage the German army, but also from the historical point of view, there had to be a purpose like that of the Maccabees. There had to be an act for history—to show that we are not going like sheep to the slaughter.

The resistance fighters were a very tight group, numbering only three hundred people. There were only three ways to be accepted: you belonged to a political youth organization, you possessed a weapon, or you had some expertise. I belonged to no youth organization and owned no weapon. But I wanted very badly to join. My only expertise was drawing, and this skill proved to be very useful. A young doctor who worked for my father had some contacts with the Polish underground, the AK, and learned from them how they manufactured fake identity papers. He needed an artist with graphic skills to draw stamps by hand, which were later imprinted on washed-out passports. I was recruited for this task. I forged one set of identity papers, and shortly afterward I was approached by Jacob Gens, who asked me to provide a false document for his relative. I did so, and the day after, I was contacted by the resistance. I was accepted into the resistance in summer of 1943, fifty-two years ago. Although we were armed and well prepared, an armed uprising never occurred in the Vilnius ghetto. The idea of resistance was not abandoned, however. Small groups were dispersed to the forests to fight alongside Soviet partisans.

On the day of the final liquidation of the Vilnius ghetto, September 23, 1943, I came to a meeting place prepared to fight. When I arrived, I saw that the few remaining machine guns were

"I THINK THAT PEOPLE ARE NEITHER BASICALLY GOOD NOR BAD. THERE ARE VERY FEW PEOPLE THAT ARE VERY GOOD OR VERY BAD. BEHAVIOR OF MOST PEOPLE IN DIFFICULT, STRESSFUL TIMES DEPENDS ON THEIR LEADERSHIP."

disassembled and ready to be transported. That's when I knew that we were not going to fight. I told my leader, Abba Kovner, that I had not brought along my forgery tools, and he ordered me to return home for them.

This was the last time I saw my mother. I told her that I was leaving the ghetto to fight in the forest. She said she suspected as much and that it was the right thing to do because a child has to survive a parent. I felt guilty about leaving her. . . . I still do. She was forty-nine years old, and she gave me her life wisdom. She said, "I know that you are going to survive. Live life to the fullest. If you have money, it can be taken away from you, and if you have children, they can die, but no one can take away a life lived well."

We went out of the ghetto through the sewers. We hurried to the forest, where we joined our colleagues who were fighting alongside Soviet-Lithuanian partisans. I remember the welcome speech we got. "We welcome you here on the base. We know that until now you have been collaborating with our enemy. You can wash your hands of this treason by fighting. There is an enormous quantity of weapons, but they are in the hands of the Germans and you have to get them."

In July of 1944 we entered the city with the Soviet army and fought in the streets of Vilnius. This was our hour: kids fighting for days with no sleep, starved but euphoric, all on the adrenaline. On July 8, 1944, the Battle of Vilnius ended. The Jewish partisans who left the ghetto in September 1943 to fight the Germans now returned to Vilnius as liberators. Very soon after that, I had a talk with Abba Kovner, who said, "Gabriel, we are organized but we are not going to stay here working for the Soviets, we are going to emigrate to Palestine to build a Jewish home and try to help other Jews do likewise." Later, in Lublin, Poland, Abba Kovner and the leaders of the resistance from other cities, including Warsaw, founded the organization called Briha, whose mission was to repatriate Jews to Palestine. I joined other partisans and worked for Briha until shortly after the war.

WE HAVE TO LEARN how to live with it. We cannot be forever at the edge of sanity. We cannot be forever afraid. Fifty years after the Holocaust, the survivors are an ever-diminishing remnant. Grass and flower, weed and tree, have spread over the mass graves; the burnt offerings of Jewish life are transformed now into memorials and museums, remembered at anniversaries, decade by decade. In a white heat, in a cold fury, in a fierce dark sorrow, we go about the business of filling in the holes, counting the absent. We struggle with what can be said, how much, by whom. Should we be silent or should we, like Ancient Mariners, attend all weddings insisting on our tale? New generations of children learn the truth: the civilized minds of the enlightenment—Goethe and Mozart, Locke and Rousseau—amid all the rumblings of liberté, egalité, fraternité, turned on the Jews and murdered them. Parisians, Poles, Viennese, and their country cousins speeded us on our way to the furnace, took our homes and our possessions. In lonely backwaters six million of us were murdered with gas and bullets, with starvation and deprivation. We've been witnesses. We haven't let the world forget. From Anne Frank to Elie Wiesel, from Martin Gilbert to Andre Schwartz-Bart, from Raul Hilberg to Jerzy Kosinski, from Aharon Appelfeld to David Grossman, the tale goes on telling itself. Every year now, another novelist, historian, photographer, finds a new corner to turn, still another story, still another voice. Our revenge is our testimony. Our testimony is among our most remarkable creations. It enables us to hold together, to go on.

There has been no forgetting despite the attempt of the revisionists, the lies of the enemies of the Jews. There is no way to deny a Shoah of such proportions. The events of the final solution remain at the center of our hearts, casting shadows across our politics, making trust difficult, complacency impossible, fueling our rage and twisting us into religious and philosophical knots. No one, neither Jew nor gentile, believes in progress anymore. No one believes that science or reason will save us from primitive bloodletting. We know that technology can serve our most sadistic impulses. What crimes may yet occur because of cyberspace?

Our nightmares are evoked by the slightest of resonances. We are offended when the memorial at Auschwitz does not include recognition of the unique Jewish tragedy forged in the flames of the death camps. We are betrayed when nuns pray at our graves. We are offended when an American president stands at the grave of our murderers and pays his respects. We are certain that betrayal lurks under the handshake of diplomats, under the smiles of our friends. We can no longer trust our G–d to save us, and so our covenant, our belief in ourselves as a covenanted people, is weakened. However, our connection one to another, to the land of Israel, is intensified by the knowledge of our calamity, by the thrust of our desire to survive as a people. We were torn apart, and in being torn apart we were forced together. We were once alone, and despite the slogans, despite the Israeli army, despite the rumored terrible weapons that may be hidden in our desert, we do not and cannot feel safe. The Jewish people see themselves as pursued; pursued by the Egyptians, pursued by the Crusaders, pursued by the Cossacks, pursued by the Inquisition, pursued by the Nazis, pursued by the Palestinians. And that image condensed, mythologized, ritualized, is part of our personal and communal consciousness; it rolls through our holiday seasons, fast and feast. It is what our children know: although they don't like the bitter tales we tell, they can't ignore us.

But of course they are further from the event than we are; as the sun comes up each morning and the earth spins on its axis, other calamities happen to other people, death and disaster come—both natural and unnatural—genocides erupt, here in Africa, there in Asia, even in the hills of Bosnia-Herzogovina. The Jewish story becomes more and more a paradigm, a warning sign, a prediction about the future as well as a story about the past. This is not anti-Semitism, this is the way of history: to absorb, to distance, to fade specifics into their outlines, to lose the details of the child's shoes, the extracted gold teeth, the attics and the barns of the righteous gentiles. History burnishes particulars, brushes them clear of individual faces, makes trends where courage or cowardice or greed or generosity once lay. Just as in the forest after the great fires, the earth sprouts green again, and in time a new forest stands; everything personal, individual, is swept away in time. The Holocaust too is in the process of being washed clean of names and faces, distanced into myth: bones that once rattled in our closets, bones of Babi Yar, of Treblinka, are settling, each year deeper and deeper into the ground.

The Nazis and their collaborators are for the most part beyond punishment; their descendants are left to feel their shame. They writhe, some with resentment, others with sorrow, under the eyes of the survivors. Each kaddish for the Holocaust dead is a reproach aimed at the heart of Christian Europe. We chase them, trying to present the laurel of guilt. They run from us to avoid being crowned. No wonder there are those trying to universalize the Holocaust, to emphasize the Poles and Gypsies. No wonder there are those who refuse to admit it ever happened. For the non-Jew the story of the Holocaust is no more than their history of shame.

Our children have begun to feel part of the whole again. They are ready to smile at friendly faces. The Holocaust says be careful, you are all—Jew and gentile—the descendants of Cain, don't count on anything, defend yourself, prepare yourself. The mark on your forehead burns. It becomes harder and harder for the gentile generations that followed the event to tolerate the taint of blame that clings to their skin. After all, they truly are innocent of any personal crime. It is hard, too, for Jews who do not remember to remember with quite the intensity, the fear, the anger, of those who were there or almost there, closer to the fire.

If only we could forgive; but we can't. Here is a story told by Rabbi Abraham Joshua Heschel: some young Jewish businessmen in high spirits found themselves in a railroad car with a small bearded man with a simple cap on his head and a sacred book in his lap. They asked the man to join them in drink and cards; when he refused, they threw his hat out the window. When the train arrived at its destination, a great crowd had gathered to greet the famous Reb Chaim of Lvov, who was known as a man of great learning and compassion. The young businessmen chased the rabbi down the platform. "Please forgive us," they said, "we didn't know who you were." "I cannot forgive you," said the rabbi, "I am the rabbi from Lvov. You did nothing to offend me. You must ask forgiveness of the little man in the car with you who had no name."

And so we cannot forgive for those who were harmed, and yet it's hard living with our communal nightmares. It's hard to pay full attention to the present. When politicians use our vulnerability and Holocaust fears to insist that we can never have peace with the Arabs, they misuse the dead. When they say "Never again" and mean "Hebron is ours," they misuse the dead. When any politician uses the Holocaust to revile other peoples, to raise the level of fear and mistrust, then we have betrayed ourselves. Our children know this. The Holocaust cannot mean that the Jews must see themselves forever as weak, forever the sacrifice on the altar. The Holocaust does not give Jews a special mandate to harm others with their own soldiers.

We are faced, whether we like it or not, with the forgetfulness that has gone on, the backing away from guilt, from pain. We are faced with the fact that this Holocaust memory, this stain on Europe's collective conscience, will be, whatever we do, altered in time. For many of us this seems like a further violation. We want to say, "Look, look, look at what you did," over and over again. But we can't because our children will lose our passion for the endeavor, and their children will lose patience with the guilt we push on them, and the entire business of what you did and how I suffered will die down to a murmur of mutual recriminations. Instead the next generation can, without forgetting, but with a less frozen eye, use its energy to know one another, to respect one another, to make their world a better place—Tikkun Olam. The writer Arthur Cohen said, "We shall become the death's head of the world, the skull through whose eyes and aper-

tures the world will see itself." We have done that, and now we have to go on. The next generation will create new Jewish thought, art, stories, politics, philosophy, midrash. They will keep the death's head among their sacred possessions, but they will not become it. They will have other things to do.

And so we come to what we can do with the Holocaust; what history with its great forward-rolling motion can do with the Holocaust. It seems that the old debate on the universality or the particularity of the Holocaust will now be resolved. The true answer is that the Shoah is both our particular story and simultaneously a story of all human beings who are smarter than they are kind, who are more inventive than they are moral, who seem to hate the other more than they love the diversity of life, who seek homogeneity when kindness and wisdom would have them search out variety. The strong will prey on the weak, and the Holocaust leaves no doubt in anyone's mind what will happen to the weak if they don't escape in time. So the Holocaust is the historical calamity of one people, the Jews, while at the same time it is the paradigm of human indifference to life, the structure of terror, that may come to others in the guise of politics, coups, ethnic cleansings, religious wars. We saw the spirit of the Holocaust in Cambodia, in Tamil, in Kashmir, at My Lai. Wherever there is a refugee camp, faces pressed against the wires, the Holocaust is there. It lives on the faces of Serbs guarding camps in the snowy mountains and in the bodies floating in the rivers at the borders of Rwanda. Wherever empathy fails, there is the Holocaust, and wherever imagination of the pain of others ends, there is the Holocaust. This is not to say that the Holocaust wasn't a unique historical event. It was. It was also a tragedy of such proportions that it became a part of the universal human design, a story that belongs to everyone. We can't keep it for ourselves; history will rip it out of our hands. We can use it, light to the darkness, to bring the world understanding: not again, not to anyone, not now, not ever. The Jews can cry fire in a world already aflame. The Holocaust is not diluted or defiled by understanding its universal aspect. It remains Jewish while it extends itself outward and connects us to humanity.

The writer and resistance fighter, survivor Jean Amery, told of seeing in December 1938 in the hills outside of Vienna a crèche with the sign on it, "All who are hungry may come and eat, all who are weary may come to rest, but the Jews will die like dogs." I often wonder what the grandson of the sign maker must think. Anger rises. Would I save the life of that grandson if he were drowning at my feet? It's a long uncomfortable wait for the Messiah.

Anne Roiphe is a writer living in New York City.

MICHAEL STOLOWITZKY | *Born* February 15, 1936 | *Birthplace* Warsaw, Poland

Passed as a Catholic boy in Vilnius; passenger on the *Exodus* | *Occupation* Director of international business development at American Express | *Current residence* New York, New York

"GERTRUDE WAS MY MOTHER. I DON'T REMEMBER MY REAL MOTHER."

I WAS BORN into a very, very well-to-do family in Warsaw, Poland. Gertrude Babilinska, who I call my mother, was my governess. She came from Danzig and was very educated.

When the Germans invaded Warsaw in 1939, my father was in Paris. He escaped to Italy and hid in the mountains. Two months before the end of the war, he was caught by the Germans and sent to Auschwitz, where he was burned.

My mother and my governess and I escaped to Vilnius, which was then in Lithuania. But, of course, the Germans captured Vilnius as well, and ghettos were established. My mother was about to be taken by the Germans when she suffered a stroke from fright and died. She was very young. Before my mother died, Gertrude promised her she would bring me to Palestine.

I grew up as Gertrude's son. We lived together in an apartment in Vilnius very near the Vilnius ghetto. I used to see how they took Jews from the ghetto. I was outside it thanks to her. There was this very large sign outside our house that said, If you are caught hiding a Jew you will be executed without a trial.

Just outside of the ghetto was the main church of Vilnius. Gertrude was Catholic, and she enlisted the priest's help in hiding me. I became an altar boy. Every Sunday, there I was, dressed in a white gown with a red apron. And all the SS from the ghetto would come to pray in this church, and I, the little Jewish boy, used to sprinkle holy water on them.

If not for this woman who told me all the time that I'm Jewish, I would never have known what Jewish is. I didn't feel Jewish. I lived as a Christian. I had curly blond hair, blue eyes. So it was very easy to pass me as a non-Jew. She actually had to convince me that I was Jewish the entire time. I didn't know what she was talking about. I was in a church. All my friends were non-Jews.

By telling me that I was Jewish she was also protecting me. Gertude would say, "If you have to urinate, don't ever do it in front of the other children. Always go to the side, because you're different." She made me aware of how careful I needed to be. She was definitely more a Jew than I was. She remembered the Jewish holidays. I never did. I didn't meet a Jew until I came to Germany in 1945, to the displaced persons camps. Maybe also at the end in Vilnius when we escaped into the forests . . .

As the Russians advanced in 1945, the bombing intensified. So we went to hide in the forests outside Vilnius. We were in this trench that was hidden underneath trees and shrubs. Up above, we could hear the Germans screaming and yelling. All of a sudden the Russians moved in toward Vilnius, and since we were on the outskirts, we met the first soldiers. One of these Russians saw our tunnel and came in with a round-barrel machine gun, ready to shoot. He was sure we were Germans. So we started screaming, trying to explain that we were a Jew and a gentile in hiding. There was a big celebration.

Gertrude took me back to her family. They said to her, "Let the boy stay here, raise him here." But she said, "No. I promised to bring him to Palestine."

We spent two years in displaced persons camps in order to go to Palestine. You had to go as a Jew from the camps, assigned on illegal boats.

We were assigned to the *Exodus* in 1947. We were 4,500 people squeezed in like sardines on a ship that was originally a Mississippi riverboat. We left France from a little port fifty miles from Marseilles. The British knew about our journey, so every day another warship joined us. There was a big battle between the Jews of Palestine and the British. The British won, and they brought us to Haifa. We were now surrounded by the entire British armada, with seven warships. And all the citizens of Haifa were standing with white sheets, waving to us. We started to sing "*Hatikvah*" on the ship. And the entire city was singing with us. I'm not a cryer, but at that moment, I cried.

We came into Haifa after a seven-day journey from France and were divided 1,500 each to three jail ships, kept like slaves down below. No air, no windows, no nothing. Normally all the Jews who came illegally they took to Cyprus. So we thought that was where we were going. But then they started talking about breakfast, lunch, and dinner, and Cyprus was an overnight trip. It turned out they were taking us back to France. We refused to disembark but sat there for six weeks and staged a hunger strike. They took us back to Hamburg.

Six months later, in March 1948, we set sail again. Only this time around the Haganah dressed us as American tourists—white pants, pink shirts, and camera cases. They even taught us how to chew gum. They put us on a luxury cruise liner and brought us into Haifa, one thousand rich Americans going on a one-day tour of the Galilee, then continuing on to Egypt on their luxury liner.

We had some kind of fabricated papers and buses waiting for us. The same English soldiers who were forcing us a few months earlier into the jail ships were standing and waving to these rich Americans. We left the harbor and never came back. I was eleven years old.

Gertrude Babilinska passed away on March 10, 1995, at the age of 94. She lived in Naharia, Israel.

I WAS BORN in 1928, in Kraków, to a big, very Hasidic family. My father was a very great man. I am the sole survivor.

In 1939, when the Germans invaded Poland, we went to live on a farm. My father believed that they would never find us there because it was in a very, very small village. There was only one Jew there, a relative of ours. My brothers shaved their beards and their *payos*, sidecurls. And we wore farm clothes. But after about six months, they did find us. And they took us to the ghetto.

Life in the ghetto was very dirty, very crowded. We spent our days just trying to get something to eat. You had to go in one long line to get a little bit of soup and then try to get in another line to get some bread. There was talk about the concentration camps—we heard about Auschwitz, about Treblinka, about the transports—but life in the ghetto was so bad that in some way it didn't matter to us if we went or not. We were in a living hell anyway.

I shared a bunk with my mother in Auschwitz. Everybody knew that if you didn't get up for roll call, they would come and take you to the gas chamber. One day, I suppose my mother was just sick and depressed and hungry and tired. She wouldn't get up. She wouldn't talk . . .

I was lying there with her. In a way I was extremely happy. I thought how nice it will be to die together. It's a wonderful fantasy for three or four minutes. But when they said, "Last call," I left my mother, knowing that when I came back she would not be there. And she wasn't. I did something that I never thought I would do. But I had to go on. I cannot explain it. I suppose I really wanted to live.

As they were transferring us from Auschwitz to another concentration camp, I jumped with some other people from the train. We escaped in our prison clothes and then at night stole clothes from some farmers. It was very, very cold. Most of the people I escaped with died on the way. You didn't dare sit down. You just had to move. I was eleven years old—the youngest of the people who jumped off the train.

After the war I was selected to come to America as a first-preference qualified orphan—you had to be under eighteen years of age and the sole survivor of one concentration camp. If you had any living relations, you didn't qualify. I arrived in the United States in September 1947.

Most of my friends in New York are survivors. They all married survivors. There are memorials in their houses. I was the only one who married an American. I never discussed the Holocaust with my husband. We just moved to the suburbs and pursued the American dream, the house born things.

"I WENT THROUGH MANY PHASES. WHEN I CAME TO AMERICA, I DIDN'T WANT ANYTHING TO DO WITH RELIGION; ULTIMATELY I CAME BACK TO IT."

AN ORDER CAME FROM THE GESTAPO to send about eighty boys from Slomnik to a labor camp by the Kraków airport. After a few months, we heard the bad news—that Slomnik and a couple of other small towns were liquidated, and the Jews taken to Plaszow. My brother Shloime was selected to remain in Plaszow. The rest were taken to the death camp of Belz.

Those of us at the airport still didn't know of the death camps and crematoriums. My reaction to my family being sent away was twofold. On the one hand, I would do everything to survive. On the other, I felt deep resignation. I lay down on the ground many times and cried to Mother Earth for bringing such bestiality upon this world.

After two months, I found out where Shloime was. I had an old piece of air force letterhead. I knew of a small hole in the barbed wire at the very end of the airport, and I figured if I was stopped, I would show them the letterhead. I arrived at the camp and told the guard I was from the Luftwaffe, and they gave me a pass to see my brother. I met a fellow Slomniker and he told me that Shloime had run away a few days ago.

Later, I found out that he ran back to Slomnik, where my sister Raizel, her husband, and their baby were. The Jewish police were now really collaborating because they were afraid for their own skins, so the few remaining Jews had to keep a low profile not to be noticed. My brother-in-law, Yossel, was a bit of a rebel and couldn't stand the injustices. He stood up for some Jews who were being harassed by the Jewish police, so they denounced him to the Gestapo as a troublemaker. In the morning, three Gestapo came to arrest him. They put him in their jeep, shot him once in the head, and threw him in a ditch.

Meanwhile, we found out that the Gestapo was planning a second deportation of all the Jews from the region; the Jews of Slomnik and about five towns were to be taken to Auschwitz or another place of no return. I was already planning an escape. I wanted to be together with my brother and sister. A few boys arranged to pay for an air force truck to Slomnik. When we got to the outskirts of Slomnik, the whole town was surrounded by Gestapo and SS. They stopped the truck, and the two soldiers driving it had a hard time explaining our motive, but they had authorization so they let us through.

Slomnik was a ghost town—no people in the streets, not even Poles. They gave us one hour to be back in the truck. It was dark already. I rushed to the house I knew my sister was in, and I found Shloime and Raizel inside. Shloime told me they planned to hide in the attic. I knew that was suicide, and I begged them to come with me on the truck. Shloime came, but Raizel categorically refused. I snuck my brother into the truck. It was dark and he lay down on the floor. The others had the same idea, so we wound up with four more passengers. We took a chance that when they counted, they wouldn't look on the floor. It was night and dark. We figured right.

The next morning, we discovered that the Gestapo had found out that some Jews had sneaked in. I had an idea to give my brother the airport letterhead I had used before. I took him to the hole in the barbed wire, and he escaped. He wound up in the ghetto. Shloime got into a group that left the ghetto every morning to work for a German building company called Strauch. Later on, the company began housing workers in a small building near the construction area. No one feared they would escape because there was nowhere to run to, except the ghetto.

I planned to escape so I could be with Shloime. Also, our work at the airport was becoming obsolete. We heard rumors that the camp was going to be liquidated and we were to be deported to Auschwitz. The hole in the barbed wire had been fixed, so the only way out was to dive underneath it and swim through the river that surrounded the camp. And so one night, I did. Nobody, not even friends, knew of my plan.

I made it to the house where Shloime and the other boys were. In the morning, I went to work with the group. We heard rumors that the Germans were building a concentration camp in the cemetery in the suburb outside the city. It was quite a large area, and they were putting up hundreds of barracks. They were talking of combining all surrounding camps into one and calling it Jerosolimska, because the road leading to the cemetery was called Jerusalem Road. In the spring of 1943 the camp of Plaszow, other labor camps, and our building of the Strauch company were moved to Jerosolimska cemetery.

The commandant of the camp was Austrian-born, about six foot three, very pale, and a real sadist. He had a villa in the middle of the camp. There were towers with guards watching twenty-four hours a day. The barbed wire was electric high-voltage, so nobody had a chance of escape. Most of the outside guards on the towers were Ukrainians who had joined the SS. As far as taking care of the Jews was concerned, they outdid the Germans.

The first few weeks, we worked in the camp putting up more barracks. It was dangerous work, working outside, because the Gestapo practiced shooting from the hills, and we were the

~Jack Tavin (left) with his brother Sol

"THEY CALLED SHLOIME'S NUMBER I SAID TO HIM, 'DON'T GO OUT.' I SMEARED HIS NUMBER, WHICH WAS SEWN ONTO HIS SHIRT, WITH DIRT SO THAT THE OTHER INMATES COULDN'T SEE IT CLEARLY. THE ONES THAT WENT OUT WERE NEVER SEEN AGAIN."

targets. Some groups were assigned to work outside the camp, like at the Kraków gas or electric company. It was better than working in the camp. At least we weren't targets. After a couple of weeks, no groups were allowed to leave the camp.

I worked in the camp dynamiting a large mountain that the Germans wanted to level. It was very rocky, and we had to drill holes in the rock, put in the explosives, and dispose of the debris afterward with wheelbarrows. Not far from where we were working was another mountain shaped like a large cone, around which was a deep ditch where the

Gestapo executed hundreds, thousands, of Jews brought from the ghetto or other towns surrounding Kraków. The Gestapo made them get down into the ditch and then shot them dead with machine guns.

One day, while I was working by the mountain, the camp commander, Goetz, was walking with his mistress and dirtied his boots. He got angry and took out his revolver and fired at me. Thank G–d he wasn't a good marksman. He fired again, and the bullet whistled by my ear. After the second shot, his mistress stopped him, and I was saved.

"IT [THE HOLOCAUST] IS LIKE A CRAZY BASS THAT IS PLAYING ALL THE TIME. I HAVE LEARNED TO PLAY THE FIDDLE ABOVE IT SO THAT THERE SHOULD BE SOME HARMONY TO MY LIFE. THERE ISN'T A SECOND, HOWEVER, THAT I'M NOT AWARE OF IT"

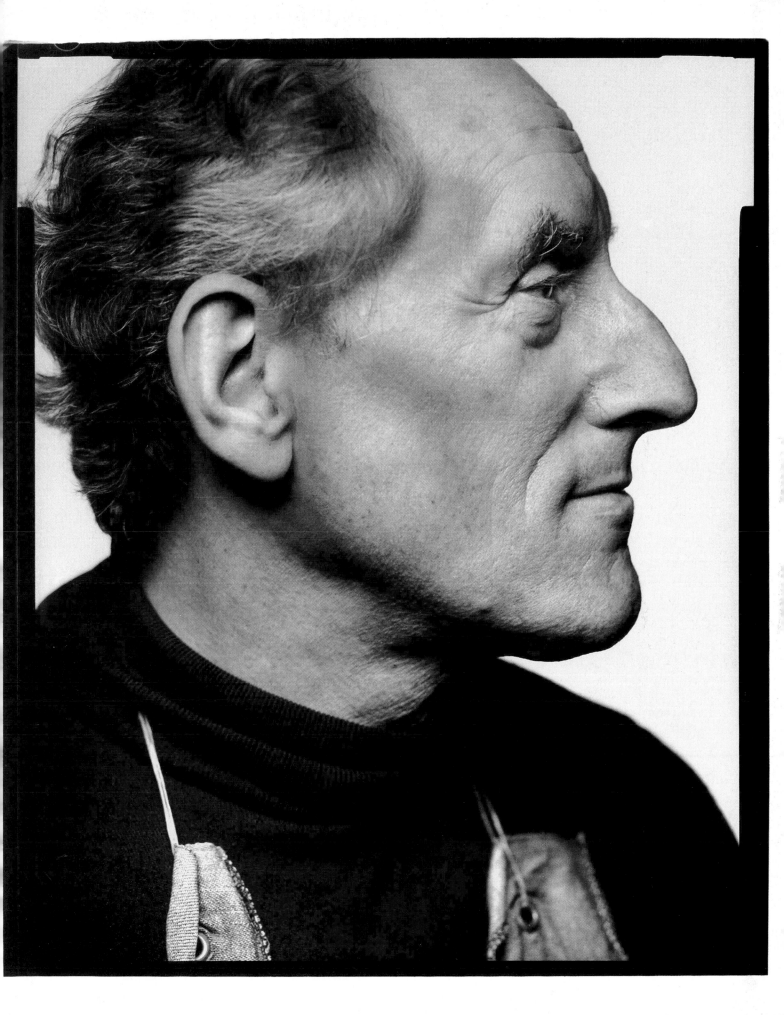

WHEN I WAS A SMALL CHILD, my parents moved back to Prague, where my father was from, and that is where I grew up. I was part of a typical Prague family—middle class, comfortable, not wealthy, rather intellectual, as Prague families of that flavor and configuration used to be. My name then was not Terna as it is now, but Taussig. We had false papers with the idea of going underground. Because my father and brother died with the name of Terna, I did not go back to Taussig after the war.

On October 3, 1941—then about eighteen years old—I was taken to my first camp, a work camp between Bohemia and Moravia, in a place called Lipa. I had been taken to a Gestapo prison twice during the summer of 1941 and interrogated in an "unfriendly" way. I was brutally beaten and fainted on both occasions, afterwards finding myself in a basement cell. Having been put into a camp may have saved me from a third interrogation. I don't know if I would have survived that one. The work in Lipa was by and large agricultural—digging ditches, working in the forest.

Lipa was dissolved in 1943, and we were shipped to Theresienstadt, where I was from March 1943 to the fall of 1944. Theresienstadt is a small fortress town that was built in the 1780s to protect Bohemia from the Prussia of Frederick the Great. It was built by Emperor Joseph II, the son of Maria Theresia, and named Theresienstadt in her honor. It was located about 40 miles north of Prague, on the confluence of two rivers: the Elbe and Eger. The Nazis realized that because of the walls and moats surrounding it, this was a place they could keep a large number of people with a minimum of guards. The Nazis moved the civilian population out of Theresienstadt and filled it from 1942 with Jews from the Protectorates of Bohemia and Moravia. Ghetto Theresienstadt became a transit camp for transports to death camps in the east. A town and garrison that before had a population of 6,000 or 7,000 at one time housed close to 60,000.

More than 120,000 people passed through Theresienstadt. Out of this number, more than 80,000 sent east. About 30,000-plus died in Theresienstadt itself. As the war was winding down, there were close to 10,000 people left. For most old people, Theresienstadt was a death sentence. It was cold, there was insufficient food, hardly any medical care, though no large-scale exterminations. From Theresienstadt, people were shipped to Treblinka and Auschwitz. In the beginning, when people died in Theresienstadt, they were buried; when it became physically unmanageable, a crematorium was built.

In 1943, the Nazis decided to use Theresienstadt as a show-place for the outside world, and because of that the Nazis allowed a certain amount of cultural activity. Books, although very circumscribed, were allowed. There were lectures—I remember very clearly Rabbi Leo Beck lecturing a whole series on philosophy—there was music, theater. I listened to and participated in just about anything I could. In fact, I started to draw in Theresienstadt. At one time, we were assigned to dig some ditches and it started to rain. We were standing underneath a shed and I happened to have a pencil and a little bit of paper and I started sketching the trees that were in front of me. From that time on, I never stopped.

I did quite a few drawings in Theresienstadt and hid them. When I was sent to Auschwitz, I gave my drawings to a woman who in turn was sent to Auschwitz and gave them to another person who gave them to someone else, and I lost all trace. In 1982, when my wife Rebecca and I went to the Beit Theresienstadt archive in kibbutz Givat Chaim Ichud in Israel, I told them my story and asked if they had any unidentified artwork. They brought out a folder with some drawings, four of them mine.

There was no attempt on my part to document. I was just drawing what was in front of me—people standing on soup lines, old people, barely moving, group scenes. This did not hold true for some of the other artists, especially the *Zeichenstupe*, a drafting office, who very consciously left a record.

Throughout my time in the camps there was an awareness of having to function after the war. The desire to have an education made us teach each other. Without books, I learned some English, mathematics—trigonometry, calculus—a little chemistry. I knew quite a bit about geography and history, so I in turn 'taught' those subjects. I remember one man from Poland who was a mathematics teacher teaching analytic geometry without a piece of paper. He would literally draw a curve in midair and go over it again and again. At some point I realized that what we were doing was not just teaching each other, but looking beyond the war. It was a kind of survival mechanism.

In Theresienstadt, I was part of what was called a *Hundertschaft*, a group of one hundred people, working mostly internally as a kind of maintenance crew—carrying lumber, digging ditches, fixing roofs, painting houses. We were assigned to different jobs as needed.

When the Red Cross was supposed to come to Theresienstadt in June 1944, I was part of a crew charged with painting the outside of houses along the designated route. The rules were clearly laid out by the Nazis; there were strict orders about what had to be done and what was forbidden. We could have just painted the houses, but we said, no, we are going to do such a good job, we will make it all letter-perfect, an exquisite stage set to make it obvious that this was in fact staged. We hoped the Red Cross would look at those houses with a skeptical eye. All they had to do was go off the prepared path, fifty yards this way or that, and see reality, see what the Nazis did not want them to see.

There was a German member, a Swiss, and a Dane on the Red Cross team. The German was obviously discounted. The Swiss member was really a Nazi sympathizer. After the war, the Danish representative said that he realized something was wrong but dared not say anything lest he endanger the few hundred Danes that were in Theresienstadt.

In the fall of 1944, there were ten big transports out of Theresienstadt to Auschwitz; Theresienstadt was essentially emptied out. I was in one of those transports. We knew we were going north from Theresienstadt, and somewhere around Dresden the train turned east. But where we were going, we didn't know. We assumed the Germans were going to use us to build fortifications. The idea of being killed outright for no other reason than being Jewish seemed illogical. Then came the arrival in Auschwitz. A few of us did not go into the gas.

We were in Auschwitz for a comparatively short time, weeks, and after another selection we were put into freight cars and sent to a subcamp of Dachau called Kaufering in November 1944. Kaufering was a group of very tough camps. They were simple, straightforward slave labor camps, where people died of starvation or exhaustion or were killed for not working fast enough. I was moved around in the Kaufering complex from one camp to another.

I was back in Kaufering camp number four when we started clearly hearing the booming of the guns at night, and were aware of the front line nearing. At one point in the middle of the night, SS guards chased us all out of our earth huts. We were all very, very weak. I could barely walk. We were loaded onto railway cars. I was very much afraid that we would be shot in those cars because the car gates were being locked.

On my way into the car, I found a piece of iron. As they were sliding the door closed, I jammed in the piece of iron, and they couldn't close the door. There was a big ruckus, but the train had to leave, so it left with the door not quite closed. I stayed near the opening. The train moved a short distance and was attacked by fighter bombers. We came nearly to a halt, and at that point, I threw a friend of mine out of the train and jumped out after him. We fell behind a tree as the planes attacked.

We had to cross a meadow to find shelter, and we were caught by a group of Hitler youth. They didn't know what to do with us, so they put us on their carts and delivered us to camp number one in Kaufering.

At that point, camp number one had been evacuated. The guards shoved us into the camp and did not bother with us anymore. I found a hole to hide in. How long I was in that hole, I don't know, it may have been hours, it may have been three days. I heard voices and looked out to see what looked like Italian soldiers. But they weren't speaking Italian. Then it dawned on me that these must be Americans, even though it wasn't what I thought American soldiers looked like. So I dug myself out a little, and somebody yelled and pulled me out. I was in bad shape, at the very end of my physical strength. I was liberated on April 27, 1945. I weighed thirty-five kilos and I was twenty-two years old.

After the war, I started out painting semiabstract landscapes and eventually realized that painting was involving me in my past. I painted landscapes with walls in them. It didn't take me long to realize that concentration camps were an ingredient in my paintings, that there was a need to express certain ideas, to deal with the past. To this day, I cannot get myself to paint visual information. I paint attitudes, emotional states, rather than physical description. But like most survivors, to some degree, I have the need to tell. And this is my way of telling.

Right after the war I made some drawings, from memory, of people between barbed wires going to a chimney, people over a shooting pit, descriptive drawings, even if not very precise. And then I just stopped, and never went back to drawing experiences of that time.

I think that I am very, very fortunate to have managed to come through with a minimum of emotional scars. I have a number of *meshugassim*, idiosyncracies, but none of them that handicap me. For example, I can't throw away shoes, and I've got to know the map, the physical layout of where I am geographically at any given time. I tend to like to plan ahead and have alternatives. If I have no control over a situation, I will be quite sure to have alternatives for handling it. Security, safety, predictability.

When you think about it, it was just a stretch of four years. Yet you can understand how people have something happen in their lives—a car accident, a brief traumatic moment—and are affected by it throughout their lives.

Three years, six months, three weeks, and two days in the camps have given me a superabundance of memories to deal with. I'm aware of the fragility of life. I'm also aware of my obligation to be a witness.

I'm here, a survivor.

"THERE WAS NO QUESTION BUT THAT WE WOULD SURVIVE THE WAR WITH OSKAR SCHINDLER."

I WAS BORN OUTSIDE KRAKÓW to an observant family. I was one of six children. We were four brothers, two sisters. My father was a tailor. He came from the now infamous city of Oświecim, or Auschwitz. My mother was a housewife. She came from Calvaria. They went to Kraków to search for opportunity.

From 1933 on, we walked to school through a hail of rock throwers. My father, who wore a thin beard, always carried a pair of scissors with him just in case he was attacked. I don't recall whether he ever used them. I think we sort of accepted anti-Semitism as the way things were.

Kraków itself was a very Jewish city. Out of a population of two hundred thousand, there were sixty thousand Jews. Religiously speaking, the Jews had freedom. The study centers, the religious schools, the Talmud Torahs, were attended, and they were growing. When the temples and schools emptied out, Jews would occupy the whole width of the street. So we felt very comfortable. And we felt that G-d would come to our aid in any times of trouble.

On September 1, 1939, the Germans marched into Poland. Within seven days or so they were in the city of Kraków. A few months later, the orders began. Jewish life ceased to exist the way it had up until this point. Jewish children could no longer attend public schools. The religious schools were also boarded up. Jewish businesses were closed or taken away. Jews could no longer walk on certain streets.

In 1941, all the Jews from the surrounding area of Kraków had to report to the ghetto. All you could take was what you could carry with you. So we took warm clothes and whatever food we had and went to the ghetto as a family. We were assigned a basement room for a family of eight. Food was in short supply. Hygiene facilities were terrible. But at least in the ghetto, somehow it felt good to be away from the cold that was being radiated at us by the non-Jews, away from the anti-Semitism.

I was picked up in the summer of 1942. Two German trucks came into the ghetto and rounded up one hundred people. The Germans would not tell us where we were being taken, what we were going to do, or whether we would come back. We were just pulled off the street. We didn't even have a chance to say good-bye to our families.

We were taken to a factory. When we arrived, there was a tall, handsome German civilian standing there. We had no idea who he was, or what sort of factory it was, but as it turned out, the man was Oskar Schindler, and the factory was the Enamel Works of Kraków. The factory had been formerly owned by Jews,

and the Germans simply took it away and gave it to Schindler.

We were the first group that was brought to the factory, aside from the previous owners. When Schindler was given the factory, he quickly found out that as a German, he could not do business with Poles. They would not buy his pots and pans. And he especially couldn't sell to them on the black market. So, clever man that he was, he simply employed the former owners, with whom the Poles were comfortable, with whom they'd done business in the past.

As Schindler looked up and down these one hundred people that were delivered, he pointed out to the SS guards that there were two children in the group and he didn't need any children. I was then fifteen, but with the war going on already for more than two years, I was undernourished and in poor health and probably looked like an eleven-year-old.

So Schindler pointed me out along with another kid my age. He must have been very naive at that time, not recognizing that by pointing us out the SS could have remedied the situation very quickly by simply removing and killing us. But luckily the SS response was, "You keep what we deliver."

From then on, I worked for Oskar Schindler. The SS picked us up from the ghetto every morning, walked us to the factory, and took us back at night so we wouldn't escape. It was a full day's work, but nobody counted hours. Of course we received no money, only food.

When we reported for work on March 12, 1943, Schindler informed us that we could not go back to the ghetto because it was being liquidated. So the one hundred of us never again returned to the ghetto. And the ghetto was liquidated. The brutality was extreme—vicious dogs hunted people out in their hiding places and tore them apart. When the Germans were through, the ghetto looked like an outdoor morgue, with bodies strewn all over streets. My family perished then.

In three or four days, Schindler was obligated to deliver the one hundred of us to a concentration camp by the name of Karkov. When we arrived at the camp, we did not yet know what had happened in the ghetto, but we could imagine it wasn't very good. Because for many weeks after our arrival at Kharkov, the Germans brought truckloads of bodies from the ghetto and dumped them into open trenches in the middle of the camp. We knew we were now in the midst of hell.

Unbeknownst to us, Oskar Schindler was working on getting us out. And after three or four months, he did get permission to take his one hundred people out. Although we had to

return to the camp in the evenings, we were able to report for work at Oskar Schindler's on a daily basis.

In 1943 the order once again changed, and Schindler was told that no Jew would be allowed to work anywhere outside of a concentration camp and that any concentration camp had to have a minimum population of one thousand. So Schindler built a camp adjoining his factory for one thousand people, with his original one hundred always the core. The SS ran it and guarded it, and there were watchtowers, but it was an entirely different experience. People were not starved. People were not killed.

This lasted from 1943 until the summer of 1944. Then the Russians gained the upper hand and began marching westward. And the decision was made—probably already after the D-Day landings—to liquidate or reduce in size the number of people in non-central camps.

There was a selection. All one thousand of us were standing in formation. Somehow I sensed that I would not be selected to remain with Schindler. So as soon as he came near me, I stepped forward—taking a tremendous chance, because the SS were there—and said very quickly in whatever German I could muster, "Herr Schindler, keine Tischler ist geblibin," no cabinet maker is left. I don't even know whether it was a fact.

But Schindler recognized me, possibly because I did some work in his office, and he took me by my arm and put me into the group of people who were to remain. All the women—seven hundred—were shipped out. Three hundred men remained, I among them.

In September of 1944 those of us who remained were also brought to Plasoff. Most of the other seven hundred people had already been shipped out to other places. It did not take very

long for the three hundred of us to be loaded into cattle cars for Gross Rosen. The situation looked very tragic. We hadn't heard from Schindler, and we were being shipped out. It looked like this was the end.

We were stripped and marched into showers. We were given a crew cut into which they shaved bare a two-inch strip from front to back, to prevent us from escaping. We were there for a few days, when lo and behold into our barrack comes an SS guard who begins to read a list of names. For us, this was extremely unusual. Up to this point, in five years of war, we had never heard our names called. We were not known by names. But here was this guard reading a list of names.

The three hundred of us were loaded on cattle cars again and shipped out to Oskar Schindler's factory, a new factory, a new concentration camp deep in Czechoslovakia. He evidently convinced the German authorities that he was doing something valuable for the army; that he was helping with armaments, and he could continue doing that in Czechoslovakia if they gave him the same skilled people he had before.

This was far from the truth, because he never did anything valuable for the armament industry back in Poland. And it was also far from the truth that we were skilled people. There was a mixture of people, of older people, women, children, certainly not skilled. Schindler also managed to get the seven hundred women out of Auschwitz, which is where they had been sent. And that's how we were once again one thousand people.

We arrived in Brünnlitz in October 1944. On May 7, 1945, Oskar Schindler called us together—by that time we were already more than one thousand people—and declared that the next day the German army would surrender to the Allied and Russian forces. And we would be free.

He told us that there were thirty revolvers with ammunition lying on his desk in his office. And that those of us who knew how to use a gun should get hold of one to defend ourselves in case stray German units came by, still trying to harm us. He also told us that the warehouses had some food and clothing and that we should appoint people to distribute this material equally among the prisoners. He stressed the word "equally."

Sometime during the night of May 7, Oskar Schindler left with his family, with his wife and his girlfriend. Some of the prisoners helped him get across the border into American-occupied Germany. On May 8, 1945, a single Russian soldier marched into our camp and told us we were free.

THE GERMANS CAME EARLY one morning–June 22, 1941. I remember all the church bells started ringing. I don't know if they were told to ring them by the Germans or if they did it on their own. . . . About two or three months after the Germans invaded, there was an order that all men from the ages of eighteen to fifty should report at 6:00 the next morning to the Jewish community building. Anyone not complying with this order would be killed. People didn't know what to do. In the end, many people went. They were marched into the forest approximately two miles outside of town. They were all killed.

After that, my father got very sick. He had been rabbi of the town for many years, and these were the people he had tended to—at their circumcisions, their bar mitzvahs, their weddings. . . . A few weeks later, he passed away.

We got through a difficult winter, and then we were told that we were being resettled. Everyone had to appear the next morning. We had a hiding place in our bedroom, underneath the floor, and a number of us went into hiding. We were thirteen people down there, including my fiancé. The Germans came into the house several times. We heard their boots and the furniture being moved, but somehow they didn't discover us. At 4:00 in the afternoon we heard a Polish neighbor say, "They must be here. There is some kind of cellar." And he showed the Germans a little window on the outside of the house that we had camouflaged. He helped them find us. They said, "Either you come out or we're going to throw in a grenade and you'll all be killed." If we had been heroes, maybe we would have said, "Go ahead." But we were ordinary people, and our will to live was very strong.

We were marched to a big place where we saw thousands of Jews. We had to sit. If anyone raised their head, the Germans would beat us terribly. I was with my mother, my fiancé, and a cousin of ours who came from another town that was already *Judenrein*. I remember looking at the Jewish cemetery and thinking, this is where they're going to leave us. I wasn't sure what they were going to do next, but I thought they would probably take us to the cemetery as they had done with Jews many times before, shoot us, and have the Polish people bury us.

About an hour later, after they rounded everybody up, they marched us to the train station. As we walked in the gutter, there were Poles standing on both sides of the sidewalk watching us. It didn't look like they were very unhappy or sorry. I felt so abandoned. It was heartbreaking to see how neighbors, some maybe even called them friends, could come and watch you like that, knowing that something terrible was about to happen. It was like a show to them; we were like bulls being led to the arena.

At the station, we were separated—all able men from eighteen to fifty on one side, all women, children, and older men on the other. There were cattle cars, not regular trains. We were pushed into these cattle cars to the point where you couldn't believe that the person you were pressing against could breathe. But there we were. They locked us in. I heard the locks, the iron bars. There were two small windows at the very top of the cars, and from the moment we were packed into the cars, I kept looking at these windows. I said to my mother, "Maybe we should think about jumping out of the window," and my mother just said, "How can we do that?"

There were two wooden planks across the window on the inside of the car, and they were wired from the outside. Somehow, we broke the planks free and started hitting the barbed wire with them until the window was open. I told my mother I was going to jump out. My mother said she wouldn't. She called over an elderly man to talk me out of it. But my quest to live was so strong that I said, "You already lived your life. I'm still young, I want at least to fight."

Somebody helped me up, and I jumped through the window while the train was moving. It's funny, I was a very sheltered child. I had never even jumped rope, and here I was jumping from the window of a moving train. I don't think I would have done it if I had thought about it or planned it, but the sheer will to survive overpowered everything. My only thought was that this is my one chance; the farther we go, the closer we are to the camps and the gas chambers. We may not have known exactly how, but by that time we knew the Germans were destroying the Jews.

The first thing I thought when I found myself lying in the field was that I wanted to go back and be with my mother. But then I heard gunshots. . . . The two people who jumped out after me were killed.

I didn't know what to do. I just lay there. Then I heard two men go by, and I thought of my fiancé. Not thinking, I called out his name. Luckily, it turned out to be two Jews who had escaped from another part of the train. They said my fiancé had been in their car. We decided to go back to town; there was nothing else we could do.

I received an illegal identity paper that said I wasn't Jewish. I bought a birth certificate signed by a Catholic priest. I thought I would use these papers to get far away from my hometown to another part of Poland, where I could perhaps survive as a Polish girl. It was a very difficult undertaking, since I didn't have any money or connections outside my town. A Polish woman who was married to a Jew and felt sorry for me wrote to her sister in Warsaw and told her that she knew a young woman who could be governess to her children. She didn't reveal to her that I was Jewish.

In Warsaw, I assumed a new identity. I became Paulina. It was very sad to walk the streets of this big city that had once been so filled with Jewish life—with beautiful synagogues and yeshivas—cleared of all Jews except in the ghetto. It was very painful to hear people say that while they hate the Germans and are sorry that they took away their country and their independence, they're glad they're getting rid of the Jews. The woman I worked for used to say, "You smell that? They're burning the Jews. I'm glad." I couldn't understand how a woman could feel this way about human beings just like her.

I was in Warsaw for about a year and a half. I met three girls and a boy from my part of Poland, also with Aryan papers. From time to time, even though it was dangerous, we would meet in the public park on our day off from work and talk, carefully, because there were always people around looking to find another Jew. But being so lonely, we defied the danger.

I accepted the customs of the people I lived with and I learned from them. I was a rabbi's daughter, but I learned their ways because I knew that I had to in order to survive. I tried to do everything they did. And they didn't know I was Jewish until the very end.

Toward the end of the war, my fiancé's sister and I were rounded up by a German military unit in Poland and put to work in their kitchen. Here we were, two Jewish girls working for Germans; they thought we were Polish!

As the Russians advanced, the Germans began to retreat. One day, an SS group arrived and asked for all the foreigners. But we had fought for so long and struggled so much, we weren't going to give up so easily. So we went to the head of the military unit and asked him to keep us. He gave us a document saying we were still needed there and he wouldn't permit our being taken away. I read later that the SS rounded up all the women and drowned them in the Baltic Sea.

None of my family was left after the war. I was absolutely alone. I didn't know at that point that my fiancé had survived. It took another year in the free world for us to find each other again. But we did find each other—through miracles, I believe.

"I WAS THE MOST SCARED CHILD THAT EVER WAS. AND NOW, NOTHING SCARES ME."

M O S H E   Y A S S U R | *Born* August 23, 1934 | *Birthplace* Iasi, Romania | Survivor of
Pogrom Iasi | Director of off-Broadway plays; former professor of drama at the Theatre Academy
in Tel Aviv and Jerusalem | *Current residence* New York, New York

WE LIVED IN NORTHERN ROMANIA, near the Russian border in a town called Iasi. A lot of Jews lived there. I was about five and a half, six years old when Pogrom Iasi took place in 1941. I remember every detail; it's so encrusted on my consciousness. My first memory of it all is of my family and other families living in the cellar of our house, where we normally kept the wine, because of the bombing. Since Iasi was kind of a border town, it was full of German troops, and we were bombarded all the time.

I remember hearing about a pogrom in Bucharest, where people were caught in the streets and beaten, killed, taken to the slaughterhouses, and put onto hooks. I remember playing in the courtyard with other Jewish children and looking for somewhere to hide. I remember being afraid of our own neighbors, who we knew were a threat. There was fear in the air; it was an unclear fear. Fear of what? We didn't know. We didn't know what beating was, we didn't know what death was. But we felt our parents' fear. They began talking about running away to Bessarabia and then across the border into Russia.

On that particular day—it was a Sunday in June, already quite warm but cool in the cellar—I heard knocks on the cellar door, and the words, "Raus! Raus!" Get out, get out! And we did, hands up. My aunt had a little baby at the time, and I remember thinking, how will she be able to raise her hands if she is holding the baby? One relative who was in his fifties or sixties took off his coat, under which he had on a Romanian uniform. "I'm not only Jewish, I'm also Romanian," he said. "I was a Romanian general in World War I." He had been quite an important officer. And the German and Romanian soldiers tore off his epaulets and gave him a good beating.

Then they took us from the courtyard into the street. Already many Jews were waiting, from other courtyards, from other houses. And we started walking toward the police station. Everybody kept saying, "It'll be okay, you know; it's only a formality." But once we got to the police station courtyard, they started shooting. People were falling down all around me, and shouting. I heard a lot of shots.

Although my parents and I had come to the police station together, we got separated. It was pandemonium. I remember holding my mother's skirt, talking to the other children, and then I got lost. The next thing I remember is people taking the corpses away from the courtyard. I was afraid to move; I thought that if I pretended to be dead, I wouldn't be killed. I remembered my mother telling me on the way to the police station, "Moishele, if you get shot, don't cry, it doesn't hurt."

I ran home. On the way, I remember seeing the street cleaners picking up people from the street, and putting them into the drums they put garbage in. I remember seeing legs sticking out of those drums. . . . Twelve thousand Jews were killed that day.

When I got home, my mother was already there. But my father wasn't. My mother was tearing a sheet and bandaging her head. She was laughing, so as not to scare me. "It's okay," she said, "it doesn't hurt." We kept waiting for Father to come home. I slept in my mother's bed that night. There were air raids during the night, but we didn't go into the shelter.

My father didn't come back.

"IN EVERY GENERATION WE HAVE A LITTLE HOLOCAUST SOMEWHERE GOING ON. IN SOME WAY WE ARE ALL SURVIVORS OF THE HOLOCAUST; YOU, I, EVERYBODY."

WHEN WE DECIDED to do a book about Holocaust survivors, we didn't realize how much it would affect our lives and in the process change the way we view the world we live in. To be able to meet these remarkable people, who let us into the most painful and darkest time of their lives, is something we will never forget. First and foremost, we would like to thank them for their courage and strength in going through their experiences with us again.

We particularly want to thank Fred Woodward for his friendship, patience, and guidance in the photo editing and design of the book to create a beautifully woven fabric of photographs and text.

We are especially indebted to Dr. Margaret Hamburg, who believed in the book right from the start and facilitated financial support at a crucial time.

We would like to thank our families for their support and love: Maurice and Carol Lee Seliger, Joel, Frank, and Lori Seliger, Anne Singer, Sam and Talia Kahn-Kravis, Bernie and Penny Kahn, and Marla Kahn.

We feel fortunate to have friends who patiently listened to all the stories about the book and gave sound advice when needed. Thank you Robert Balsom, Susan Cohen, Tom Connors, Eva Fogelman, Robin Gibbs, Itzik Gottesman, Hal Goldberg, Simon Helegua, Ellie Hamburger, Daisy Houli, Lelani Hill, Laurie Kratochvil, Gary and Judy Liberson, James Newberry, Ruth Obernbreit, Jodi Peckman, Debbie Penzer, Jane Praeger, Susan Plotner, Val Wasserman, Jann Wenner, Ronnie Weyl, and Bob Zdon.

In the studio we couldn't have made it without the following people's hard work: especially Cathy Weiner and Josh Liberson, as well as Liza Gurall, Abbey Gennet, Brian Long, Eric Delphenich, Alex Martinengo, Nick Young, and Mel Hill.

A special thanks to Yoomi Chong and Eric Siry for their typographic assistance and to David Szanto at Arcade.

We are grateful to the Holocaust Museum for their constant help in finding people to interview, especially Sarah Ogilvie and her volunteer, Michel Margosis. Florence Smerldi of The Blue Card was similarly helpful.

Anne Edelstein, our agent, got us our chance to see the book published and worked through all the problems with us.

The following people helped with the interviews: Betti Forma, Karen Hefler, Sara Melson, Michelle Litvin, Michelle M. Hedges, Ann Forstater, and Kathy Hinkley.

Technical assistance and supplies were generously donated by Ilford Corporation, Polaroid Corporation, Bishop Studio, Candid Litho, Kelton Labs, and Megargee/van der Linde Lab.

A final thank you to Brennan Cavanaugh, who put it all together, and Nate Kravis, who proofed everything and listened to everything.

Mark Seliger and Leora Kahn
July 1995

This book was partially funded by a grant from The Nathan Cummings Foundation.

Royalties from this book will be donated to The Blue Card, a non-profit agency that makes grants to Holocaust survivors and their children.

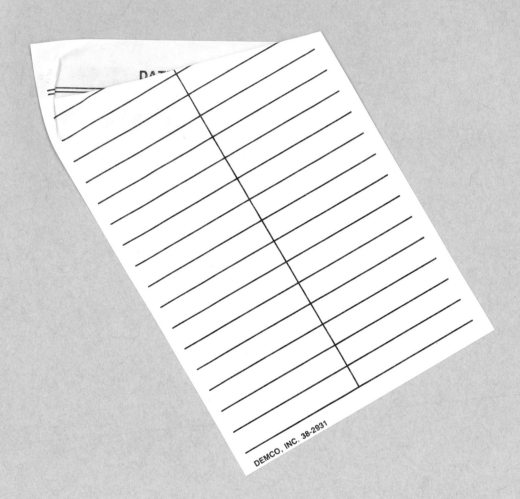

DEMCO, INC. 38-2931